THE LEON B. POULLADA MEMORIAL SERIES
Delivered at Princeton University

This public lecture series was established by the family and friends of Leon B. Poullada (1913–1987), a United States career diplomat whose service took him to South Asia, Afghanistan, and Iran. Mr. Poullada retired with the rank of ambassador and then earned a doctoral degree in Politics and Near Eastern Studies at Princeton University. Thereafter, he devoted almost two decades to teaching and scholarship. In recognition of his diplomatic and scholarly contributions, especially his long association with the peoples of Persian and Turkish languages and cultures, this public lecture series under the auspices of the Program in Near Eastern Studies, Princeton University, invites eminent scholars in Islamic studies, broadly defined, to present the results of their scholarship in a form meaningful to the nonspecialist.

THE INAUGURAL
LEON B. POULLADA
MEMORIAL LECTURE SERIES

AFGHANISTAN:
The Failure of Revolutionary Islam

by
OLIVIER ROY

Centre National de la Recherche Scientifique (CNRS)
Paris, France

AFGHANISTAN:
From Holy War
to Civil War

OLIVIER ROY

THE DARWIN PRESS, INC.
PRINCETON, NEW JERSEY USA

Library of Congress Cataloging in Publication Data

Roy, Olivier, 1949–
   Afghanistan : from holy war to civil war / Olivier Roy.
      p.   cm.
      "Inaugural Leon B. Poullada memorial lecture series on
   Afghanistan: the failure of revolutionary Islam"—CIP galley p. 2.
      Includes bibliographical references and index.
      ISBN 0–87850–076–6 (alk. paper) : $24.95
      1. Afghanistan—Politics and government—1973– 2. Islam and
   politics—Afghanistan.   I. Title.
   DS371.3.R69   1994
   958.104'5—dc20   94–18404
                                                                   CIP

The paper in this book is acid-free neutral pH stock and meets
the guidelines for permanence and durability
of the Committee on Production Guidelines
for Book Longevity of the Council on
Library Resources.

Published by
The Darwin Press, Inc.
Box 2202
Princeton, NJ 08543 USA
Tel.: (609) 737–1349
Fax: (609) 737–0929

Printed in the United States of America.

CONTENTS

Maps 7–10

Introduction 11

CHAPTER ONE:
  Islam and Society in Afghanistan: An Overview 17

CHAPTER TWO:
  From Fundamentalism to Islamism 27

CHAPTER THREE:
  The Mujahidin and Political Islam 41

CHAPTER FOUR:
  Jihad as an Ethical Model 61

CHAPTER FIVE:
  Afghanistan and the World Islamic Revival 77

CHAPTER SIX:
  War and Social Changes 103

CHAPTER SEVEN:
  Afghanistan: From Ideology to Ethnicity 117

Glossary of Political Parties and Religious
  Organizations 125

Bibliography 129

Index 133

(Plates follow page 96)

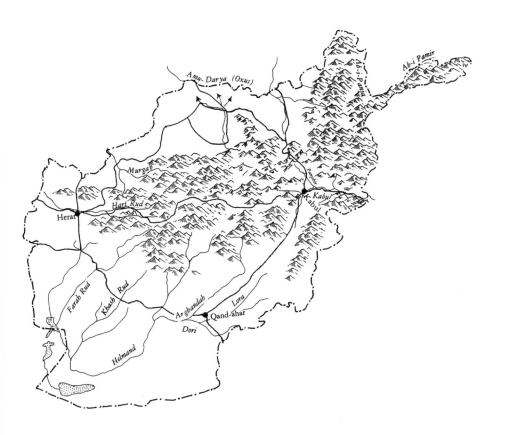

Map 1. Geography: roads, rivers, mountains, and major towns.

Map 2. Provinces (after 1964).

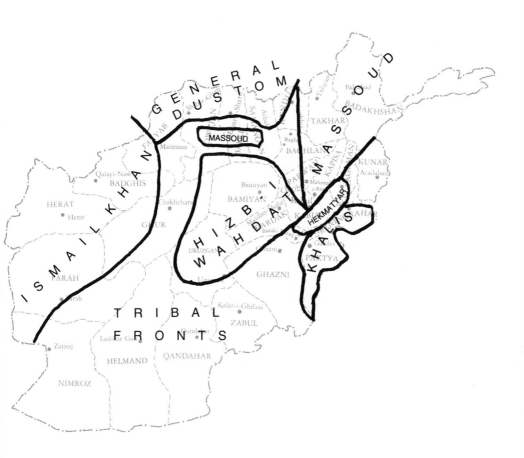

Map 3. Areas controlled by principal guerrilla leaders (1993).
[The end of the jihad had two contradictory consequences for the
political map: In tribal areas (Pashtuns, Baluchis, and Nuristanis),
political parties as such have lost their grip, and administrative duties
are performed by traditional tribal assemblies (*jirga* and *shura*). Elsewhere, we see the emergence of four political forces with ethnic and
territorial bases: the Jam'iyyat (with Ismail Khan in the west, Massoud
in the northeast), the former Communist Uzbek militias of General
Dustom in the north, the Shi'i party Hizb-i Wahdat in the center,
and the mainly Pashtun Hizb-i Islami-ye of Hekmatyar, around Kabul.
A Hizb-i Islami (Khalis) party remains in the east.]

☰ Baluchi	⸛ Ismaili	⦚ Turkmen
⧄ Pashtun	⊞ Kirghiz	⫽ Uzbek
■ Hazara	⧄ Nuristani	⸛ Tajik

Map 4. Ethnic groups across frontiers.

INTRODUCTION

THE PAST TWO DECADES have witnessed the irruption on the international stage of a an Islam that is both political and ideological. To the traditional fundamentalism, as ancient as Islam itself in its demand for a return to the Qur'ān and the shari'a, has been added, with authors such as Hasan al-Banna, Sayyid Qutb, and Abu al-Ala Maududi, a very political reading of religious action. People now speak of an Islamic state, an Islamic party, an Islamic revolution. Militant Islam has moved to the left and raised the banner of its struggle against imperialism; this movement seeks to ensure social justice and establish a just economy, thus offering a third direction: one between capitalism and socialism.

This Islamist ideology has served as a slogan for militant, radical, and sometimes revolutionary political movements in countries such as Egypt, Iran, Afghanistan, Algeria, to name only a few. During the eighties, one could wonder whether Islam constituted the dominant ideology of political movements in the Muslim Third World. Aspiration toward a genuinely Islamic society crystallized into a millenary populism that lent substance and direction to social movements as well as to a bewildered intelligentsia. This same aspiration made its peace with the Westernizing of political discourse modeled on the great ideologies of the twentieth century, especially Marxism, with the cultural identity of the Muslim peoples, and with the search for a new spirituality. Islamist political ideology furthermore provided an organizational framework for political action by adapting the Leninist model of the party to the structure of a traditional mystical *tariqat* or *sufi* brotherhood.

The war of resistance in Afghanistan is one example of this Islamic militancy. In a very conservative and traditional society, it was Islamic parties led by young intellectuals educated (usually

11

in the sciences) in state universities who were able to mount the armed and political resistance. One might mention the two Afghan mujahidin leaders Ahmad Shah Massoud and Gulbuddin Hekmatyar, both former engineering students.

The failure of political Islam is flagrant. If the mujahidin did succeed in forcing the Soviet Army out of their country, however, they did not manage to establish a new society. Instead, traditional Afghan society has returned, with its ethnic and tribal divisions, but also with its concept of power centered around networks of clientele and personal allegiances. If Massoud succeeded in building an effective military machine, it was by abandoning ideological references and falling back on a compromise between traditional Afghan society and the purely juridical fundamentalism of the mullahs.

This defeat of political Islam in Afghanistan is by no means due solely to the special characteristics of that country. In our view, the Afghan mujahidin movement serves as a particular case study of the failure of political Islam in general. This failure has occurred at two levels. On the first, the ideological matrix put in place by the modern founders of fundamentalist political Islam such as al-Banna, Sayyid Qutb, and Maududi has impeded the establishment of genuine political institutions because it depends on the virtues of a charismatic religious leadership. The question of the amir, the charismatic chief, is central: The organization of political Islam depends upon a man, not upon a political structure; this was not the case with the Communist parties behind Third World national liberation movements. The ethical questions override political considerations. The good leader, the good militant, and the good citizen are "good" only insofar as they are good Muslims, endeavoring to imitate the virtues of the Prophet. With even the slightest weakening of the ethical model (or with a reappearance of traditional society's cleavages or simply if ambition and greed win over the militant's faith), the political system is emptied of its substance and no longer functions.

In fact, and this is the second level of failure, Islamist ideology is unable to think in terms of the society's sociology: Ethnic identities, tribal segmentation, and power relationships are thought of as ethical shortcomings, forms of ignorance or sin. Nevertheless, these sociological realities return, and win, over ideology. Throughout the Muslim world, *umma* is an illusion, never a political reality. Everywhere, Islamic parties are cast in the same mold as the nation-states they condemn; the Front Islamique du Salut (FIS) is profoundly Algerian, as the mujahidin are above all Afghans, and the Iranian Revolution is a national one. Everywhere, from Algeria to Afghanistan by way of Iraq and Iran, ethnic identities remain essential to understanding the workings of politics, including those of Islamic parties. The only truly Islamist revolution has been the Iranian one, whose failure is today apparent, both in its capacity for exporting revolution and for building a just and prosperous society. Everywhere else, in Afghanistan as in Algeria, the Islamists' victory, on the contrary, underscores the permanence of native sociological and historical realities that their ideology has endeavored to suppress but are nevertheless encountered in the practice of everyday politics.

In my book, *Islam and Resistance in Afghanistan*, written in 1985, I tried to explain how the Afghan mujahidin movement was a merging of the reformist Muslim fundamentalism that had pervaded Afghan history since the early nineteenth century with the contemporary brand of political Islam (or Islamism) generated by the theories of Hasan al-Banna and Abu al-Ala Maududi.

In the present book, I try to assess the impact of the Afghan mujahidin movement as a case study of the success and limits of the Islamist political framework. Islamism undoubtedly enabled the mujahidin to cope with modern warfare: It provided an ideological incentive. The mujahidin forced the Soviets to leave Afghanistan in February 1989. But the shortcomings of their movement appeared as soon as the Soviets left. The Communist regime was able to last an additional three years by playing on ethnicity and on the traditional segmentation of Afghan society. This policy backfired in the spring of 1992, when the mujahidin succeeded in taking control of Kabul, precisely because of ethnic rifts within the Communist regime. Yet, neither in the liberated areas nor in Kabul have the mujahidin been able to establish an

Islamic state that might be a modern model for Muslim societies. Islamization means only application of shari'a in matters of personal law: veils for women and a ban on alcohol. All other levels (politics, economy) are played according to either traditional (ethnic segmentation, patronage) or Western patterns (capitalism).

Does this mean that my original analysis was flawed, that I had failed to see the traditional society that stood behind Islamist ideology? No, because the Islamist momentum has in fact altered the sociological and political patterns of Afghan society, but not in the ways it was supposed to. It has modernized society in the sense that it brought into power an educated and urban elite and has, paradoxically, accelerated the process of ethnic consolidation along linguistic lines. Islamist parties contend for state power, whereas more traditional leaders are attracted only to local leadership. Finally, Islamists have linked Afghanistan with the main political movements of the Muslim world (Saudi Wahhabis, Muslim Brothers, etc.). Even so, there is definitively no new model of an Islamic state.

An analysis of present-day Afghan society discloses at least two social models: a tribal model (a classic one from an anthropological point of view, albeit one open to varied interpretations) based on the concept of segmentary groups defined along a pyramidal genealogy; and a dynamic model of ethnic identity, subjective and relative, that one must understand in terms of a social context highly influenced by the political moment. The former model is relevant to Afghanistan's tribal zone, essentially those occupied by the Pashtuns, in the east and south; the latter, to an understanding of groups living in the north and west. Rather than apply these two anthropological models rigorously, I have endeavored to find a common thread that might explain the totality of this society and what is essentially an evolving situtation.

Distinguishing between tribal and nontribal zones is not critical to an understanding of the main topic of this book, namely, the re-traditionalization of political Islam. The key here is to view "solidarity groups" from the perspective of political loyalties that go above and beyond such concepts as "tribe," "clan," and "segmentary group." Likewise, the reader must take "solidarity space" to mean an "area of operations" (for a network of allies) rather than a fixed geographical territory.

I have described Afghanistan as seen through the eyes of a social scientist, in terms of social events as I saw them happen, without particular reference to a pre-defined theoretical framework.

In closing, I should like to add that this study is the fruit of more than eighteen months spend living and doing research among the Afghan mujahidin, from 1980 to 1988.

CHAPTER ONE

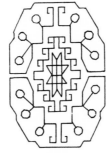

ISLAM
AND SOCIETY
IN AFGHANISTAN:
AN OVERVIEW

Islam in Afghanistan

Dividing Islam into schools and trends is regarded with suspicion by most Muslims. But it is a necessity if one wishes to understand the current situation in Afghanistan. Among Afghan Sunnis, one can distinguish the following features:

• "Popular knowledge of Islam,"[1] which does not represent a school or a trend but the way Islam is experienced, integrated, and practiced by the mainly uneducated population to express a *weltanschauung*. This "popular Islam" should not be opposed to "orthodox Islam," because the population does not make a distinction between the two and recognizes the superiority of the knowledge of the ulama. It is the way orthodox Islam and certain other practices (magic, superstition) are combined and experienced as a whole.

• Scriptural Islam of the Afghan ulama, which is based on the Sunni Hanafi school, heavily influenced by orthodox Sufi schools, as it was taught in the Indian subcontinent madrasas (Deoband), after the Shah Waliullah reformist movement. This school of thought was dominant in all Afghan madrasas before the war.

1. I borrow this expression from Nazif Shahrani's "Local Knowledge of Islam and Social Discourse in Afghanistan and Turkistan in the Modern Period." In fact, the popular perception of Islam could not be called a "school" nor a trend, because ordinary people do not try to systematize or impose what they know to be superficial knowledge and because they acknowledge that the ulama know better. I agree with Shahrani's criticism of one of my early papers: "Popular Islam" should not be separated from "scriptural Islam," but should be seen rather as the way nonclerics and little-educated people receive a popularized Islam.

• A reformist movement, also having its source with the Shah Waliullah movement, but more rigorist, established in British India in the early nineteenth century and called "Wahhabi" both by British observers at that time and by traditional Hanafi mullahs. The movement that embodies this trend is the Indo-Pakistani "Ahl-i-Hadith," whose influence in Afghanistan came through local, "frontier," madrasas and crept into Afghanistan during the past decades through local and rural mullahs. This is not a political Islam, but a true fundamentalist movement. Its goals are to return to the basic tenets (Qur'ān and Sunna), to reject accretions, borrowings, syncretism, and, to some extent, mysticism.

• A political Islam borrowed entirely from the writings of Abu al-Ala Maududi, Hasan al-Banna, and Sayyid Qutb, which was introduced into Afghanistan in the 1960s by certain professors of the State Faculty of Theology who had been educated in Egypt. Ideology and organizational structures are borrowed from the Muslim Brothers movement and the Pakistani Jama'at-i Islami.

• Wahhabism, *stricto sensu*, which appeared during the present war through Saudi money and missionaries.

The war brought both frictions and integration among these trends. Under an active Arab patronage (Saudi and Muslim Brothers from Jordan, Sudan, and Egypt), an endeavor has been made to combine the last three trends into a coherent brand of neofundamentalism. This movement had some success among political parties based in Peshawar and among refugee camps and contributed to an "Islamization" of Afghan society. Arab patronage failed, however, to convert the Afghan mujahidin movement into a coherent, united, and effective political organization. Its influence has been religious and cultural. In the political field, the real influence has been that of Pakistan's Inter-Services Intelligence (ISI), which was in charge of channeling American-financed weapons to the mujahidin. It generally supported the same radical and fundamentalist groups as did the Arabs.

The Shi'a, who make up about 15 percent of the Afghan population, kept aloof from these trends and underwent a process of revolutionization and Iranization through the influence of Iranian scholars like Ayatollah Khumayni. In Hazarajat, before the rise of these young mullahs, traditional Islam used to mix popular customs and reverence for the *sayyid*. But a recent political reform movement, under the influence of mullahs trained in Iran or Iraq, spread from urban Shi'i communities (not necessarily Hazara) to the Hazarajat from the 1950s on. This politicization ended after the Soviet invasion, because mullahs and Islamist intellectuals succeeded in excluding traditional Hazara notables, mainly landowners, from local power. After a civil war among themselves, involving pro-Iranian radicals and conservatives, Afghan Shi'a split along ethnic lines: The bulk of them, the Hazara, came under Iranian patronage (constituting the Hizb-i Wahdat in 1989), whereas most of the Kizilbash accepted Pakistani support.

The Traditional Segmentation of Afghan Society

It is commonly alleged that Afghan society is a tribal society and that the state has never really been able to control the countryside. It is better to say that Afghanistan is a segmented, but not always tribal, society. Following three patterns of segmentation, namely, from the smallest unit to the largest, we find: the *qawm*, then the tribe, and at the top the ethnic group. This configuration gives the central state some room to maneuver. At the local level, the political game consists of competition between qawms or between tribes. In this case, the state is perceived as a referee among opposing groups trying to obtain state support against their rivals. At the national level, the competition for power is mainly among ethnic groups. Here, by contrast, the state has always been seen as a tool of Pashtun domination over other ethnic groups. These complex sociological patterns are the key to explaining political life in Afghanistan, but they also play a large role in the evolution of the whole area, because most Afghan ethnic groups live beyond Afghan borders.

Every Afghan, at least in the countryside, is supposed to belong to a segmentary group called a "qawm." Qawm is the term used to designate any segment of society bound by solidarity ties. It could be an extended family, a clan, an occupational group, a village, etc. It does not refer to a corporate group; it is used situationally, in apposition to other qawms. For example, in a Pashtun village, the qawm of a tribesman is his clan when speaking to his fellow tribesmen, his tribe in comparison to the other tribesmen, the Pashtun ethnic group in relation to the other groups. But there is not necessarily a symmetry between different qawms. In the same Pashtun village, a craftsman not belonging to the tribe will call "qawm" his occupational group, and a mullah claiming to be a sayyid (descendant of the Prophet) will qualify the sayyids as forming a qawm. This shows that qawm could not be linked solely to a "tribe." One must speak about "tribalism" *stricto sensu* only for the southern and eastern Pashtun areas. Tribal organization assumes that qawms (here better translated as "clans") fit into a pyramidal organization according to a more or less legendary genealogy. Tribalism also assumes a specific common law, ideology (embodied in the *pashtunwali,* or "Law of the Pashtuns"), and institutions (the *jirgah,* or "tribal council"). Contrary to the Kurds and the Baluchis, for example, the Afghan Pashtun tribes are acephalous: competing big families contending constantly for preeminence.

But there are qawms even where there is no symmetric, segmented group defined according to a pyramidal genealogy. In a word, if a clan or a tribe are qawm, all qawms are not tribes or clans, especially in nontribal central and northern Afghanistan. The answer to the question "What is your qawm?" might differ not only from one part of Afghanistan to the other, but even for a same person according to the context: It could be a clan in a village, this village by opposition to others in the same valley, the valley by opposition to the rest of the province. Qawm is based on kinship or client/patron relationship. It is a solidarity group, which protects its members from encroachment by the state and other qawms, but it is also the area of competition among contenders for local supremacy.[2] Qawm is a network, not a territorial unit. Different qawms could coexist in one village.

2. For the definition of qawm, see Pierre Centlivres, *Un Bazar d'Asie Centrale,* pp. 158-59; Whitney Azoy, *Buzkashi: Game and Power in Afghanistan* pp. 31–32; Olivier Roy, *Islam and Resistance in Afghanistan,* chap. 1.

It is a mistake to translate qawm by "ethnic group." Superficially, it might appear that this is the correct definition (when one group is compared with other groups), but, when asked, it is never the first acceptation given by the responder. By the way, the question remains: What is an ethnic group in Afghanistan? How to qualify a Sunni Persian-speaker of Badakhshan Province claiming to be of the "Baluchi" qawm, although he does not speak a word of Baluch, has no memory of any Baluch ancestry, and does not retain any feeling of solidarity with the Baluchis of Baluchistan? What about Uzbek and Persian speakers having emigrated from Central Asia and claiming both to be of the "Samarkandi" qawm, after the city of Samarkand? We will see later that a new sense of ethnicity based solely on language is now emerging in Afghanistan, but formerly language was not the primary criterion.

If one uses language as the basis for identity, the main ethnic groups, by order of demographic importance, are: Pashtun, Tajik —that is, Sunni Persian speakers—Uzbek, Turkmen, Baluchi, and Nuristani. The Hazara, who speak Persian but are Shi'a, should be considered as an ethnic group here, in this instance religious criterion (added to some physical features) superseding the linguistic one.[3] Even this definition of "macroethnic" groups based on linguistic criteria is not very relevant as far as primary identities and local politics are concerned. The spoken languages do not describe clear-cut ethnic groups or groups with a common sense of identity and a will to express themselves politically.

3. Most statistical figures on Afghanistan are biased or simply incorrect. The monarchy claimed that Pashtuns made up 51 percent of a total population of 17 millions. In fact, both figures should be lowered: the Pashtuns might constitute from 40 to 45 percent of a population not exceeding 15 millions in 1970. The number of "Tajiks" depends on the definition of a "Tajik." If it includes all the Sunni Persian speakers, they might constitute 35 percent of the population. But most of the figures given by anthropologists artificially divide Sunni Persian speakers into many different "ethnic groups" (as "Sunni Hazara, Aimaq, etc."). The Shi'a (also Persian speakers) claim to be 30 percent of the population. They might constitute 15 percent. Turkish speakers might constitute about 7 percent. Others are Baluchi (200,000), Nuristani (100,000), Pashay, Ismaili mountaineers in the Pamir (50,000), Sikhs and Hindus (10,000), Kirghiz (5,000), Gujar, etc.

Ethnic identity is a social and dynamic process: A Pashtun tribesman, for whom tribal affiliation is more important than language,
will not call a local Pashtu-speaking craftsman "Pashtun," because
craftsmen are excluded from tribal genealogies. A sayyid (that
is, a descendant of the Prophet Muḥammad), is seen as belonging
to the qawm of the "sayyid," but not to the ethnic group among
whom he lives and whose language he speaks. The majority of
Sunni Persian speakers (like the Aimaq of Central Afghanistan,
the inhabitants of Herat City, on the Iranian border, and even
of Kabul) have not, at least until recently, called themselves
"Tajik," although this term is applied to them by ethnologists
and journalists. They identify themselves through their local
qawm or through the language they speak (using the term *farsiwan,* or "Persian speakers") without any ethnic connotation. On
the contrary, some Turkish (but not Uzbek) speakers will call
themselves "Uzbek" in order to be identified with a better-known
and more numerous ethnic group. Ethnic groups are more a
construction, in which politicization might play a role, than a
spontaneous and basic identification.

As for the Pashtun, while they all agree that the power in
Kabul "belongs" to them, they do not have the sense of forming
a "Pashtun nation-state": Pashtun nationalism is not developed
among the Pakistani Pashtun (called Pathans), and tribal affiliations everywhere supersede ethnic identity. Two Pashtun tribal
confederations have been competing for power over Afghanistan
since the foundation of the nation in the eighteenth century: the
Durranis, who provided the ruling dynasties from 1747 to 1978,
and the Ghilzays, who constitute the majority of both the People's
Democratic Party of Afghanistan (PDPA) and the Peshawar-based
parties. (The 1978 coup was seen as the Ghilzays' revenge against
the Durranis.) A third Pashtun group is composed of the eastern
tribes on the Pakistani border; these tribes have never been united
in a political confederation and have always retained a fierce sense
of independence; yet, they are influential both in the PDPA and
in Peshawar.[4]

4. Among these tribes, some are situated both in Afghanistan and Pakistan, like the Mohmands, Afridis, Waziris; others are purely Afghans, like
Jadrans, Jajis, Khugiani, Safis, etc.

The terms designating leaders and notables usually refer to informal areas of power. The khan is the traditional leader for a qawm; the malik is any leader who acts as a mediator between his group and the state. The power of the khan is based on property and wealth, hospitality, and generosity. He is usually in competition with other khans, or would-be khans. The malik exists only in relation to the state: He is the interface, the representative of the traditional society vis-à-vis the state, which in turn entrusts him with certain state functions. Thus, he helps with the census; in refugee camps, he distributes passbooks to members of his group; he may levy taxes for the state, recruit labor on its behalf, and select youths for military conscription. This position allows the malik to institutionalize his function and to give it a permanent and profitable aspect.

* * * * * *

This overview indicates that Islam, sociologically speaking, is composed of many different groups and conveys different meanings according to varying social or political contexts, even though Muslims of Afghanistan—as Muslims elsewhere throughout the Muslim world—would resist such compartmentalization and would claim to see Islam as a unity.

The pattern of complex segmentation that constitutes Afghanistan's social system can be explained by outsiders in other than Islamic terms. The resulting contradictions, whether of Afghan self-image or of an outsider's efforts to understand Afghan society, provide the necessary background to the argument presented in the coming chapters.

CHAPTER TWO

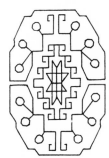

FROM
FUNDAMENTALISM
TO ISLAMISM

THE AFGHAN MUJAHIDIN movement is a part of the Islamic revival that has characterized the Muslim world since the 1960s. Its sole originality has been sociological. This movement has become the only contemporary revivalist Muslim movement to take root among peasants and was a consequence of the Communist coup of April 1978 and of the subsequent Soviet invasion in December 1979, which provoked a general Afghan uprising. Before assessing the distinctive developments in Afghanistan, one must study mainstream "fundamentalist" thought, keeping in mind that the debate about what is "political Islam" is confined to the world of Sunni Islam. It is also to some extent the same in Cairo, Karachi, and Afghanistan. Only the center of Shi'i political Islam, Iran, provides the exception. The Shi'i Hizbullah of Lebanon does also, to some extent, but with less impact beyond Lebanon's borders.

Whatever the trends, there has been no original Afghan thinker or writer on Islam and politics. Islamist mujahidin parties are explicitly taking their political inspiration from contemporary political Islam, and their journals print either translations or paraphrases from Arab or Iranian sources.[1] In order to discuss the impact and failure of revolutionary Islam, we need to compare mujahidin practices with the blueprint of an Islamic society, or

1. For instance, the Jami'yyat-i Islami journal *Misâq-i Khûn* used to print extensive translations from Hasan al-Banna, Sayyid Qutb, Muhammad Qutb, and Abid Tawfiq al-Hâshimi. The texts we use in this chapter are to be found either in mujahidin journals or are translated in Persian and available in the cultural offices of these parties, such as *Jihâd in Islâm* by Maududi and *Fi Zilâl al-Quran* by Sayyid Qutb; the latter has been translated by Burhanuddin Rabbani, head of the Jam'iyyat-i Islami-yi Afghanistan. In discussing the ideas of *Zilâl*, I quote extensively from the commentary made by Olivier Carré, *Mystique et Politique*. Among the main Muslim Brothers texts that appeared in *Misâq-i Khûn*,

29

state, as it appears mainly in the writings of Sayyid Qutb and Maududi and in the mujahidin press. If the Afghan mujahidin did not actually engage in theoretical and doctrinal thinking, they had more than their share of the action. They waged a nine-year war against the mighty Soviet Army, and, at the time of the Soviet withdrawal, the mujahidin controlled about 80 percent of Afghan territory.

Afghanistan is a good testing ground for Islamism in action, but with two caveats: 1) The fact that the Afghan mujahidin movement took root among the peasantry makes it susceptible to the traditional segmentation of Afghan society—tribalism and ethnicity; 2) the small number of people comprising the Afghan intelligentsia undoubtedly made it more difficult for them to conduct a political program reaching deep into traditional society, even though intellectuals played an important role as leaders of the Afghan peasantry against the Soviets and the Communists.

Old Practice and New Trends

Islamic fundamentalism is nothing new in the Muslim world; the term is commonly used to describe any appeal to make Islam the sole rule of social life. The term denotes in fact various attitudes and ideologies that, although sharing a common theme ("Islam encompasses all aspects of social life"), differ not only in their historical and sociological backgrounds but also in what is seen as the cornerstone of an Islamic society. Does "Islamization" of a society mean:

---

we may mention: *Da'wat-i Islami* ("Islamic Preaching"), a translation by Hemati of "Letters of Imâm Hasan al-Bannâ" (April, June, December 1365/ 1986), and a regular chronicle entitled *Nizâm-i siyâsi dar Islâm* ("Political Order in Islam"), translated into Persian from Abid Tawfiq al-Hâshimi.

A history of the Egyptian Muslim Brothers appeared also in the issues of the first year of *Misâq*: "Jonbesh-Hâ-ye-Islâmi dar pîch-e wakhm-e târikh" ("Islamic Movements in the Turmoil of History"), by Dr. Sayyid Muhammad Musa Tawana.

1) The implementation of the shari'a by the ruler, whoever he is;

2) A personal return to strict religious practices and a "purified" faith through preaching, the spread of which would create, almost automatically, an Islamic society; or

3) The need to establish first a political Islamic state, if necessary through revolution and violent means?

There is, of course, no clear-cut separation between these trends. Implementation of the shari'a, for example, is the common denominator for all. The first trend, which characterizes the history of the Muslim world, generally took root among ulama and mullahs, and sometimes has been embodied in specific doctrines, like Wahhabism in Saudi Arabia; but it is also the outlook of traditional mullahs, whatever the century or the school of thought they belong to. By contrast, the belief that a society can be truly Islamic only if a vanguard of faithful "born-again" Muslims endeavors to create an "Islamic state" is a modern idea that has been developed during this century by laymen, not mullahs. This second trend, which appeared in the thirties, is embodied by the Muslim Brothers and the Jama'at-i Islami. During the 1960s, more radical thinkers like Sayyid Qutb in Egypt and Ayatollah Khumayni during his exile in Iraq developed new ideas that were to give birth to a third revolutionary, violent, and radical trend. This trend has been embodied in the Iranian Revolution (1979) and in some splinter groups from the Muslim Brothers, such as the Jihad movement in Egypt, the "Liberation Party" (Hizb al-Tahrir) in Jordan and Palestine (whose leader, Taqi al-Din Nabhani, is a former Muslim Brother), and the Hizb-i Islami in Afghanistan. The mainstream Muslim Brothers, however, oppose the radicals on two key points: the duty to topple existing regimes through revolution and violence and the right to brand present Muslim rulers as "infidels."[2]

I would call "fundamentalism" strictly speaking the mere will to return to the shari'a, without questioning the nature of state and society, and "Islamism" the theory according to which

---

2. Radical Islamists used to add to the five pillars of the Islamic faith a sixth one, the "absent obligation," or jihad, which could be conducted against "bad" Muslims; see Gilles Kepel, *Le Prophète et le Pharaon*, pp. 184ff.

an Islamic state should be established through political means by destroying the existing regimes and changing the present society, which is said to have become "infidel" again, even if the majority of the population is culturally Muslim. By stressing the need to think of Islam in political terms, Muslim Brothers and Jamaʿat-i Islami are "Islamists," but they generally avoid defining precisely what is an Islamic state and what are the ways to seize power. This ambivalence is at the core of the failure of political Islam.

Fundamentalism

Fundamentalism is thus the will to return to what are believed to be the true tenets of Islam as practiced in the time of the Prophet Muḥammad and his early followers and, above all, to regard the shariʿa as the cornerstone of society, encompassing all aspects of life, from personal worship (*ʿibadat*) to judicial institutions. Such religious reformist movements have recurred throughout Muslim history, reacting against what its spokesmen regard as dereliction from Islam. Two historical fundamentalist movements, which appeared during the eighteenth century, are of particular importance for Afghanistan today: Wahhabism and the Shah Waliullah school of thought in India.[3] Although all fundamentalist movements are grounded on implementing the shariʿa, they could be, as far as other fields of Islamic knowledge and practices are concerned (e.g., philosophy or mysticism):

1) Either traditionalist, accepting Sufism (such as the Deobandi school of India) and even the cult of saints (the Barelvis);[4]

2) Or scripturalist reformist, seeking to purge religious practices of borrowed elements like Sufism or even, as with the

---

3. The two movements are sometimes confused in the Indian subcontinent and in Central Asia under the name of Wahhabism. See Qeyamuddin Ahmad, *The Wahabi Movement in India*.

4. On religious revivalism in the Indian subcontinent, see Barbara Metcalf, *Islamic Revival in British India: Deoband*.

Wahhabi and Ahl-i Hadith movements, refusing to acknowledge the existence of the four orthodox schools of law (Hanafi, Maliki, Shafi'i, Hanbali).

Such a dividing line is important for the social rooting of this movement but has no direct political consequence. Strongly fundamentalist movements are not necessarily radical in politics. The Ahl-i Hadith accepted British rule in India, and the Wahhabis often allied with the British in the Middle East and with the United States after the 1950s.

For the fundamentalists, any ruler who is a Muslim enforces the shari'a, protects the interests of the Muslim community, and fights against "innovation" (*bid'at*) and foreign influences is a good ruler, however he acceded to power. Hence, the support of the Wahhabis for the Saudi dynasty, although there is nothing about "Muslim kings" in the Qur'ān. These fundamentalists, usually clerics, never claim political power for themselves, but they demand authority to enforce the shari'a or at least to pass judgment on the conformity to the shari'a of the laws passed by a ruler. This leaves room for secular politics: the manner of access to power, or even the way this power is exercised (i.e., through *ta'zir* and *qanun*, decrees and laws passed by the rulers on matters not relevant to the shari'a or for the sake of public welfare).

There is really no theory of the meaning of politics. The genesis of power is thus secular. It may be brought about by mere force (General Zia's 1977 coup d'état in Pakistan), or by tribal consensus (for instance, the present Saudi ruler was chosen by the consensus of the princes, not by the ulama), or by any other way. There is little or no reflection on what an Islamic constitution should be. Mere implementation of the shari'a is supposed to take care of all political needs. Paradoxically, this exclusive insistence on shari'a leaves room, as we have already mentioned, for political secularism; the power game obeys its own rules, not those of the shari'a for which the ruler, beyond the veil of divine decree, is always the de facto wielder of power. That explains why, in Afghanistan, traditional clerics have almost never risen against any regime prior to the Communist coup of 1978 (except against Amanullah in 1928), even though King

Zahir (in power from 1933 to 1973) and President Daoud (1973 to 1978) were doing their best to secularize and Westernize Afghan society, while giving lip service to Islam and the shari'a.

Islamism

New ground was opened in the late nineteenth century. Reformist thinkers (known as *salafis*)—whose archetype was Jamal al-Din al-Afghani (d. 1896) who, this time, did not come from the ranks of traditional clerics—sought to assess the reasons for the weakness of the Muslim world vis-à-vis a triumphant Christianity.

The salafi trend gave birth, in the twentieth century (from the 1930s onward), to two very close, although geographically distant, movements: the Muslim Brothers, founded by Hasan al-Banna in Egypt, which spread into the Arab world, and the Jama'at-i Islami in the Indian subcontinent.[5] The ideology of the Jama'at-i Islami is based solely on the writings of Abu al-Ala Maududi (1903–1979); the Muslim Brothers' ideology proceeds from many different sources, ranging from the founder, Hasan al-Banna (1906–1949), to his more radical disciple Sayyid Qutb (1906–1964), who in fact is closer to Maududi. Both organizations have been inspirers and mentors of the Islamist Afghan mujahidin.

Both advocated a return to what is claimed to be the "true" tenets of Islam, but both introduced several decisive new concepts that signalled a rupture with traditional fundamentalism. For Maududi and Qutb, it is a religious duty to:
   • Break with present society, considered corrupt and ignorant (i.e., in a state of *jâhiliyya*);
   • Establish a "Party of God" (Hizbullah);
   • Install God's sovereignty (*hâkimiyya*), that is, an Islamic government;
   • Promote social justice (instead of mere conformity between deeds and shari'a.)

For them, there were no true Islamic states in history except at the time of the Prophet and the Four Rightly Guided Caliphs,

5. For a general survey, see Edward Mortimer, *Faith and Power*.

the immediate successors to the Prophet. The shari'a is not the only requisite to qualify a state as Islamic.[6] The head of state, or *amir al-mu'minin* (commander of the faithful), should embody the virtues of Islam and be chosen according to Islamic precepts. All institutions, not only personal status law, should be based on the Qur'ān and the Sunna.

Both Maududi and Sayyid Qutb insisted that a true Muslim society could be established only after a radical break with the present society, which is in a state of *jâhiliyya*; no compromise could be accepted: "Islam is a revolutionary ideology and program which seeks to alter the social order of the whole world and rebuild it in conformity with its tenets and ideals."[7] For Sayyid Qutb, contemporary Muslim society has regressed to the same state of unbelief that existed before the Prophet Muḥammad.[8] What should be achieved is an "Islamic revolution" (*thawra islamiyya*)[9] not only against existing regimes but also against traditional jurisprudence (*fiqh*), which, because it is purely formal and casuistic, accommodates the present society and is an obstacle to establishing a true Islamic "order" (*nizam*).[10] The rupture with present society supposes an individual choice: True believers must join the "Party of God." The "Islamic party" should not be a political organization like other parties. It should bring together the "born-again Muslims," the "brethren," under the authority of an amir; such a party is a community of the faithful, a vanguard, a countersociety, a mirror of what the umma should be. Within this framework, the brethren endeavor to live *hic et nunc* according to the rules they want to implement in the whole society.

Islam means a new and total order, reshaping the whole society and implementing social justice.[11] For instance, in the

6. Mere implementation of shari'a could mislead people into believing that the state qualifies as Islamic, according to Sayyid Qutb, quoted in Olivier Carré, *Mystique et Politique*, p. 165.

7. Maududi, *Jihâd in Islâm*, p. 5 (text written in 1926).

8. On Qutb and jâhiliyya, see Carré, *Mystique et Politique*, pp. 207-10.

9. See Carré, pp. 142, 143, 174.

10. Carré, p. 165.

11. Abu al-Ala Maududi wrote, "Islam is not merely a religious creed or compound name for a few forms of worship, but a comprehensive system that contemplates annihilating all tyrannical and evil systems in the world and

Afghan Jam'iyyat-i Islami party's guidebook, the first principle
to be learned by any member is "Islam is the name of this total
and all-encompassing order [*nizâm-i jâme' va kâmil*] that organizes
all aspects of life." There follows a list of these aspects: "state,
fatherland, government, nation, moral standards, death, justice,
culture, laws [*qânun*], science, judiciary [*qazâ'*], materialism and
spirituality, acquisition and wealth, jihad and preaching [*da'wa*],
politics and opinion [*mafkûra*]."[12] There is no room for any secular
politics. This all-encompassing power of God over society is called
hâkimiyya by Maududi and Qutb and *tawhid* by Imam Khumayni,
but the expression *tawhid* has been used also by Sunni thinkers.[13]
The goal is to redefine the social fabric as a whole, not just apply
shari'a prescriptions casuistically. That involves changing the
individual, society, and the state. Hâkimiyya is all-encompassing
not only because an Islamic constitution has established new laws
and institutions that will produce good Muslims but because the
faithful have given up all their worldly concerns and agreed to
rely totally on God. According to Muhammad Qutb:

> Islam in its general and wide sense means that man should
> give himself up to God, surrender his soul completely to him
> and leave everything, however small, in His hands.[14]

Such a society is a totality but is not totalitarian because no
person or institution can embody Islamic rule, neither man nor

---

enforces its own program of reform, which it deems best for the well-being
of mankind." *Jihâd in Islâm*, pp. 16-17.

12. *Osûl-e Ba'yat va Mas'uliat-há-ye 'ozu* ("The Principles of the Oath of
Allegiance and the Responsibilities of the Member") of Jami'yyat-i Islami of
Afghanistan, p. 4. This sort of enumeration is frequent and often replaces an
explanation.

13. A series of articles under the title *Nizâm-i syâsi dar Islâm* ("Political
Order in Islam") by Abid Tawfiq al-Hâshimi, translated into Persian, appeared
in the Jam'iyyat-i Islami journal *Misâq-i Khûn*, where both terms are used;
hâkimiyya is to be found, among other references, in the Hizb-i Islami statutes,
p. 93; "the party . . . must cooperate . . . with all the systems and governments
that are dedicated to implementing Islamic hâkimiyya."

14. In Azzam, *Islam and Contemporary Society*, p. 1.

the state. The ruler, God, is not acting within the society; the norm is not reduced to the political order, but is above it. The Law and the State are one. The state is a means, not an end. The law-sayer (not maker) is subordinated to the law and can be criticized in the name of the law.

The term hâkimiyya is not in the Qur'ān; it is a neologism, as was critically pointed out by Hasan al-Hudaybi, the leader of the Muslim Brothers, in 1969.[15] Nor, of course, for that matter, does the word "ideology" appear in the Qur'ān. It is interesting that expunging "secular" elements from the social and political sphere, like *ta'zir* and *qânun*,[16] is done under the auspices of non-Qur'ānic concepts, which are obviously borrowed from the great Western ideologies of the twentieth century.[17]

Why should the "Muslim Party" seize state power? According to Maududi, it is because "it is impossible for a Muslim to succeed in his intention of observing the Islamic pattern of life under the authority of a non-Islamic system of government."[18] It is clear that the final aim of society, as with Aristotle, is to allow the human being to achieve his highest spiritual nature.

How to seize power? Revolution is necessary because the present society is in a state of jâhiliyya; but does this mean striving to topple existing regimes, even if they are Muslim? Or should one endeavor instead to bring the ruling elite back to true Islam? The debate about *takfîr*, that is, declaring a Muslim to be an unbeliever, is the watershed between moderate and radical Islamism.[19] If takfîr is religiously lawful, then violence and revolution are religious duties. For radical Islamists, one should kill

15. Carré and Michaud, *Les Frères Musulmans*, p. 98.

16. See al-Hâshimi's article in *Misâq-i Khûn*, no. 19, p. 39, which states "in a tawhid society there is no room for ta'zir and qânun."

17. See Said Amir Arjomand: "This meant the arrangement of readily accessible maxims constituting the sources of the Islamic tradition, the Qur'ān, the sayings of the Prophet and the Imams, in accordance with a new pattern suggested by the Western totalitarian ideologies such as communism and fascism" (*The Turban for the Crown*, p. 97).

18. Maududi, *Jihâd in Islâm*, p. 19.

19. For a review of the problem with its historical background, see Emmanuel Sivan, *Radical Islam*.

a ruler who claims to be a Muslim but does not rule according to Islam.[20]

Political radicalization occurred in Egypt (as expressed by the radical groups Takfîr and Jihad and by the assassination of Sadat), Syria, and Afghanistan. Meanwhile, the mainstream Muslim Brothers were less vocal in the political field and played the role of a Muslim Opus Dei (a Catholic lay order recruiting among elite laymen) by influencing the ruling circles. Such was more nearly the case in Jordan as well. This policy of influence rather than of activist radicalism has been followed by the Pakistani Jama'at from its inception.[21]

In Sunni circles, by contrast with Shi'a, Islamism did not make a breakthrough among the clerics and thus remained confined to the middle class and lay students who staffed the campuses.[22] Although there was almost no connection between the Shi'a and Sunni militant groups, the impact of the Iranian Revolution gave a boost to radical Sunni elements, at least until the outbreak of the war between Iraq and Iran that put an end to the dream of erasing the gap separating Shi'ite and Sunni. Only a few splinter Sunni Islamist groups put into practice the Iranian phraseology concerning revolution and took violent action (the assassination of Sadat being a major example). Nevertheless, the Iranian Revolution had such an impact on Afghanistan that even conservative groups adopted a revolutionary terminology, such as the Harakat-i Inqilab-i Islami (the Islamic Revolution Movement), which is in fact a clerical and conservative group that does not oppose the return of former King Zahir. Among all Islamist parties, the terms "Islamic revolution" and "Islamic ideology" became common.[23]

20. See G. Kepel, *Le Prophète*, p. 184ff.

21. The Jama'at-i Islami has never been part of the Muslim Brothers movement, but, in ideological and organizational terms, the two are very close. Sayyid Qutb was a great admirer of Maududi, and the writings of the leading authors of both organizations were translated and distributed by the sister organization.

22. For a sociological study of a radical Islamist group in Egypt, see R. Hrair Dekmejian, *Islam in Revolution*, p. 106.

23. See, for example, *Osûl-e Ba'yat*, p. 1: "Jamiat members are fighting

At the end of the 1980s, the failure of Islamist movements to take power led them to adopt a more conservative attitude, stressing re-Islamization of the society more than revolution. This change allowed them to bridge the gap that existed between the "established" clergy and the "revolutionary" vanguard. Islamists ceased to frighten the population by advocating revolution. In fact, they are returning to the mainstream teachings of the Muslim Brothers, to a sort of "neofundamentalism."

To sum up, traditional fundamentalism is the mere wish to see shari'a being implemented, whatever the political power; Islamism is the transformation of Islam into a political ideology, stressing the need to reshape society from above, after having taken state power; and neofundamentalism is what remains after the failure of Islamism. Behind the political rhetoric about an "Islamic state," there is nothing more than an authoritarian change of everyday life and habits, leaving intact the political power game, the economy, and the geostrategic constraints. But this is not a mere circle. Islamism has wrought a new elite and has contributed to the weakening of traditional notables and culture. In its way it is a part of the process of modernization, but not the answer to the challenge of modernity.

The Shi'a Exception

Only Iranian Islamists have succeeded in taking power and establishing state control. Except, however, for a short period following the coming of Khumayni to power, when the Iranian Revolution had a momentary but tremendous impact among Sunni radical groups, there have been no organic and few personal connections between the founders of the Iranian Revolution and the theoreticians of the Muslim Brothers and the Jama'at (although Sayyid Qutb was widely read among Iranian thinkers).[24] The ideology

---

for the sovereignty [*ḥākimiyyat*] of the eminent teaching of Islam and for implementing the Islamic revolution"; "members of JIA should be absolutely sure that their ideology [*ideolozhi*] and thinking are a completely Islamic ideology and thinking," p. 2.

24. Arjomand, *The Turban for the Crown*, p. 9.

of the Iranian Revolution embodied the utmost degree of politicization of Islamic fundamentalism, thus converting Islam into a political ideology. This radicalization and ideologization of political Islam attracted the bulk of the Islamic opponents of the Shah, probably because a significant part of the clergy, under the guidance of Ayatollah Khumayni, supported and fueled the new ideas. The main difference between Maududi and Qutb, on the one hand, and Khumayni, on the other, is that the former are more concerned with society than with the state. Their model is Madina, the first community living under the direct guidance of the Prophet himself.[25] They think in terms of community, not constitution or institutions.

Contemporary Shi'ism is better equipped to cope with political institutions than is Sunnism. There is a potential for institutionalizing power in the persons of ayatollahs who can interpret the law. There is a process of designating them, through cooptation. The Khumaynist concept of *velâyat-i faqîh*, the "mandate of the jurist," has in fact accomplished the junction between a transcendental order and worldly politics. The actual religious guide could reveal the law; he is a (religious) lawmaker and not just a law-sayer as for the Sunni. The guide is a mujtahid; he can interpret divine law.

This movement, however, has not created a theocracy. Instead, it has secularized political Islam: For Khumayni, "revolution" (*inqilâb*) could supersede the shari'a.[26] In fact, in Iran, the Islamist movement is as much an offspring of contemporary Third World liberation movements as of centuries-old Islamic fundamentalism. There is a primacy of the political order over the devotional order.[27] The present evolution of Iran, which is beyond the scope of this study, is, however, consistent with the basic thesis that has been presented in this chapter: Politicizing Islam leads to its secularization.

25. Carré, *Mystique*, p. 181.

26. This was stated by Imam Khumayni in January, 1989, criticizing a sermon made by the then president of the republic, Ali Khamene'y, who evoked shari'a to limit the powers of such revolutionary institutions as the "Revolutionary Guards": See *Iran Yearbook 1989-90*, pp. 9–13.

27. "There are a hundred more Qur'ānic verses on social problems than on devotional questions": Khumayni, *Pour un gouvernement islamique*, p. 12.

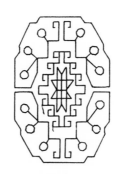

CHAPTER THREE

THE MUJAHIDIN
AND
POLITICAL ISLAM

THE SUBJECT OF THIS CHAPTER are the mujahidin, who see Islam as an all-encompassing social and political system. We shall leave aside traditional tribal leaders and Westernized politicians. Among the mujahidin, we may distinguish four trends, which may sometimes overlap:

    1) Fundamentalist Sunni clerics

    2) Sunni Islamists (split into moderate and radical camps)

    3) Shi'a Islamists

    4) The so-called Wahhabis or "neofundamentalists"

1) Fundamentalist Sunni clerics. Fundamentalist Sunni clerics may be found in almost any party, but they constitute the bulk of the traditionalist and clerical Harakat-i Inqilab. They are fundamentalist in the strict sense of the word: They advocate implementing shari'a but are ready to accept any ruler who is a Muslim (Afghanistan's former king, for instance). They have neither a viable political organization nor a political conception of society. The main split among them is between traditionalists, who accept sufism and philosophy, and scriptualist reformists, who recently joined the so-called Wahhabi movements.

2) Sunni Islamists. In Afghanistan, Sunni Islamists play the same role that Muslim Brothers do in Arab countries, although they do not use the term "Muslim Brothers" (*al-Ikhwan al-Muslimin*) to describe themselves, the term *ikhwan* being considered derogatory since the government has used it to discredit the mujahidin.[1] The hard core in each of the two most important mujahidin parties, the Jam'iyyat-i Islami (JIA) and the Hizb-i

---

1. *Afghan News,* the JIA newsletter edited by Muhammad Ishaq, protested against the use of the term "ikhwan" by the Voice of America to denote Islamists because of the radical meaning attached to this term in Afghanistan (*Afghan News,* January 1991).

Islami-ye (HIH) (although now antagonists), is made up of former activists who, ten years before the 1978 coup, built up Islamist networks at the campuses of Kabul's universities and in several urban clerical circles. These circles were founded by theology professors, such as M. Niazi and B. Rabbani, who when studying at al-Azhar in Cairo adopted the ideas of the Egyptian Muslim Brothers. They read and translated Hasan al-Banna, Sayyid Qutb, and Muhammad Qutb, who, along with Abu al-Ala Maududi, have provided the main textbooks for the Sunni Afghan mujahidin Islamists; these activists, however, never developed an original ideology or political system.

The split that occurred during the 1960s and 1970s in Egypt and the Arab world between moderate and radical Muslim Brothers (who followed Sayyid Qutb's principles) had its equivalent in Afghanistan. The Muslim Brothers, who in Afghanistan are a moderate group, constitute the bulk of JIA and of an HIH splinter group (led by Mawlawi Yunus Khalis). Burhanuddin Rabbani, head of the JIA, is a typical representative of this trend. He is a cleric but has taught in the Faculty of Theology, not in the private and more traditionalist madrasa. He studied at al-Azhar in Cairo, where he encountered the Egyptian Muslim Brothers. He translated Sayyid Qutb's *Fi Zilâl al-Quran* ["In the Shade of the Qur'ān"] into Persian, but he also quoted extensively from Muhammad Qutb, brother of Sayyid Qutb, who was less revolutionary-minded than his brother. Rabbani had close ties with Shaykh Talmasani, the moderate *murshid*, or leader, of the Egyptian Muslim Brothers from 1973 to 1986. He opposed takfîr (i.e., considering as non-Muslim those Muslim rulers who do not establish an Islamic state),[2] and he calls his political organization a "society" (*jami'yya*), not a "party" (*hizb*). There is no

2. "A Muslim who recites the *kalima*, acts according to it, puts in practice the religious prescriptions, cannot be said to be an infidel because he expresses an opinion or commits a great sin." *Osûl-e Ba'yat*, Article 17.

In the next pages, we will constantly refer to two booklets that are published by the two Islamist Afghan parties and express both parties' statutes and members' duties: for Jam'iyyat, *Osûl-e Ba'yat va Mas'uliat-há-ye 'ozu* (henceforth, *Osûl-e Ba'yat*), and for HIH, *Mas'uliat-há-ye 'ozu* (henceforth, *Mas'uliat*). Congruences and differences between them are highly instructive.

"cult of personality" around him. The motto of the party is "The Qur'ān is our Constitution," but emphasis is put on individual religious reform, not on establishing the rule of a party or of an amir: An Islamic society exists when everyone acts as a good Muslim, beginning with the rulers and administrators.[3]

Afghanistan's radical Islamists are almost all in the Hizb-i Islami led by Hekmatyar. Sociologically, most of them have a secular background. They refer to the same ideological sources as the moderates but adopt the most radical reading of Sayyid Qutb and Maududi, preferring the stricter Hanbali school of law to the Hanafi, which predominates in Afghanistan. Their party has a rigid, almost Leninist organization, and its statutes insist on discipline, obedience, and allegiance. The amir, focus of a cult of personality, holds strong authority over party members, justified by his right to *ijtihâd*.

3) Shi'a Islamists. Shi'a Islamists from the Hazara ethnic group are predominant in the Sazman-i Nasr and Sepah-i Pasdaran organizations now united into the Hizb-i Wahdat (Party of Unity), whereas non-Hazara Shi'a dominate the Harakat-i Islami (based in Kabul and Kandahar) and Hizbullah (based in Herat). Afghan Shi'a Islamists have borrowed their political ideas from Iranian thinkers such as Ali Shariati and Ayatollah Khumayni. Leftist mottos and ethnic-based nationalism were widespread among the young Hazara intellectuals, although they used an Islamic rhetoric extensively, both under the influence of the Iranian Revolution and because of the need to cloak their radical opinions with a religious mantle in order to reach the clerics and a conservative peasantry.

4) Wahhabis, or "neofundamentalists." In Afghanistan as in the Indian subcontinent and Central Asia, the term Wahhabi has been used since the nineteenth century to designate any scripturalist, reformist movement that, contrary to the traditional

---

3. *Osûl-e Ba'yat*, p. 17: "There is a government with an Islamic form when its members are Muslims, put into practice their own Islamic duties and religious obligations, and do not disobey Islamic rules." This definition is very conservative. In the next sentence, the text makes it perfectly lawful for an Islamic state to employ non-Muslim experts.

fundamentalism of the mullahs, rejects the four orthodox schools of law and strongly opposes Sufi (mystical) practices.[4] In Pakistan, this trend was embodied in the Ahl-i Hadith organization, whose madrasa in the 1950s trained Afghan mullahs from Badakhshan and Kunar provinces.

Recently, this trend has made a comeback due to Saudi influence. The Saudis supported Abdul Rabb Sayyaf, an Afghan assistant professor of theology trained in Mecca (as opposed to the bulk of Kabul University's Faculty of Theology professors, who were trained in Cairo). Sayyaf briefly headed one of the alliances that was supposed to merge all the mujahidin movements, then founded his own organization, the Ittihâd-i Islami (Islamic Union). At the same time, some independent "Wahhabi amirates" have been created by local mullahs in Badakhshan (at Argo) and in Nuristan (Mullah Afzal, in Barg-i Matal). The two brands of Wahhabism have thus been merged.

The Party and State: The Blueprint

Afghan Islamist mujahidin have borrowed heavily from the Muslim Brothers in terms of actual organization and political programs. But an additional element must be noted: For ten years (1965–1975), the intelligentsia that would later head the Islamist mujahidin movement lived in closer (even if hostile) contact with local Marxists than did the Muslim Brothers in Egypt. Thus, there has been some penetration of the Leninist party organizational model, here probably stronger than anywhere else in the Muslim world. The following comments on the conceptions of party and state are taken in their broad lines from the Muslim

4. See text of Abdullah Ezzam in the journal *Al-Jihâd* (in Arabic, no. 56, June 1989). Abdullah Ezzam, a Jordanian Muslim Brother established in Peshawar, protested against the derogatory use of the term Wahhabi to qualify the movements supporting the mujahidin. Interestingly enough, he said that this use was a plot of "Western media, Kabul Radio, Sufi marabouts, and the Voice of America...."

Brothers and are illustrated by examples from the two Afghan Islamist parties, the JIA and the HIH.

The Party: Political Instrument or Brotherhood? Sayyid Qutb and Maududi advocated the establishment of an elite "Islamic party," headed by a guide (*murshid*) or an amir (Maududi's term). For Maududi, this party should use state power to achieve the Islamization of society.[5] "An International Revolutionary Party is born to which the Qur'ān gives the title 'Hizb Allah'. . . . Muslim is the title of that international revolutionary party organized by Islam to carry into effect its revolutionary programme, and jihad refers to that revolutionary struggle."[6] For Maududi and Qutb, this party is not so much a political party in the modern sense of the word as it is the vanguard of the umma, or, more precisely, the rallying of those who have personally experienced a return to Islam and have created, in the midst of a corrupt society, a "community of the pure." It is, in a sense, a "micro-umma."

Their conception of the party is at the intersection of two traditions: that of a Sufi order, in which the aim is gradual, personal achievement of perfection under the tutelage of a guide, and the Leninist tradition, in which the party is an instrument for taking power.[7] The guidebooks of the Afghan mujahidin parties stress not only obedience to the party's principles, but also "mental confidence" in the leader (*etminan-e zahni*). A Sufi expression, *'ashq varzide nesbat be islâm* ("to be in love with Islam"), is even used, along with a reference to tasawwuf, or Sufism.[8] These lines make it clear that the "party" is perceived less as a political instrument for seizing power than as a community where the born-again Muslim is brought up, educated, and enjoined to keep his new faith in a hostile, ignorant, and perverting modern

5. Maududi, *Jihâd in Islâm*, p. 18: "Hence this party is left with no choice except to seize state authority."
6. Maududi, *Jihâd in Islâm*, p. 17.
7. For quotations of Sayyid Qutb on the party, see Carré, *Mystique*, p. 125.
8. *Mas'uliat*, n.d., p. 76 for "love" and p. 83 for tasawwuf.

world. Nevertheless, the party is not a clerical organization: Its
members are usually laymen who are engaged in professional
occupations and who sometimes lack even basic knowledge of
Islamic theology and law.

The HIH's hierarchy envisaged by this concept of "community" posits four levels of affiliation and responsibilities, corresponding to the degree of commitment, education, and training
of its members, with each stage carrying specific duties. The
stages are:

1) Sympathizers
2) Members
3) "Pillars"
4) *Shura-ye markazi* (Central Council)

The latter elect the amir, assisted by an Executive Committee
(*komite-ye ejrâ'ya*).[9] The leader is assisted by technical committees:
political, general secretariat, students, military, information, etc.
The levels of "initiation" are explicitly compared with a mystical
and Sufi initiation: "This party is from the moral point of view
the vanguard based on spirituality [*rûhâniyat*] and Sufism [*tasawwuf*]."[10] The guidebook gives two models of personal commitment: Sufism for spiritual achievement and military for discipline
and organization. The combination of both is necessary to "edu-
cate" the new member, who should purify his soul in order to

9. This organizational scheme was borrowed from the Egyptian Muslim
Brothers, which has the following ranks (from bottom to top):

1) *Halqa* (cell): initiation to the Sunna and to the teachings of al-Banna.

2) *Al-Usra* (family): at least 5 years. One reads *Al-Bay'at* of Maududi,
gives 5 percent of his income, and pledges allegiance to the local leader.

3) Working Brother (active member), chosen by the leader, has learned
the Qur'ān, has responsibilities.

4) *Majlis al-Shura*: Appointed by the leader among active members.
We have compiled this organizational scheme from different sources, including
personal interviews. For a similar structure among the Palestinian Muslim
Brothers, see Mohammed K. Shadid, "The Muslim Brotherhood Movement
in the West Bank and Gaza," pp. 658-82.

10. *Mas'uliat*, p. 83. In Afghanistan, the Persian term *rûhâniyat* does not
mean clergy as in Iran; rather, it denotes the spirituality and sanctity of the
Sufi pir.

achieve a "spiritual" (gnostic) education (*tarbiha-ye 'erfâni*) (page 83 of *Mas'uliat*). The first three levels of affiliation correspond to three "stages" of initiation, which are called:

1) *Ta'arruf* ("seeking knowledge"), in which the candidate should acquire knowledge of the society, of preaching, and of Islamic literature;

2) *Takvîn* ("genesis"), in which the candidate should acquire absolute obedience to the party's principles, in order to purify himself;

3) *Tanfîz* ("implementation"), in which the candidate is able to implement the party's policy.

A party member is called *rafîq*, "comrade," as in the Communist party. Absolute obedience, confidence, and loyalty to the leadership is mandatory and is cited as proof of discipline and also of self-abnegation. According to some oral sources, only members who were active prior to the Communist coup of 1978 could be members of the Central Council. Once elected, the amir appoints an "executive council" of 13 members and may nominate 21 new members to the Central Council. Interestingly, in this guidebook, the stress is put on the education of the member rather than on the organizational framework: The way members are chosen and promoted as well as the extent of the amir's power are not explicit in the party's statutes. In fact, the actual organization of HIH has always been shrouded in some mystery.

JIA membership statutes employ almost the same terminology and definitions as the HIH, with less emphasis on the amir and on discipline. It also acknowledges in theory three stages of militancy:

1) *Mo'arefî* ("introduction"), exposition of the party's principles among the masses (page 25);

2) *Tanzîm* ("organization"), which combines "spiritual education" (*tarbya-ye 'irfânî*) and a paramilitary organization in cells (*haste*), page 27;

3) *Tanfiz* ("implementation"), which is also a personal achievement.[11] In fact, this theoretical hierarchy was not, at the

11. *Osûl-e Ba'yat*, pp. 25-27.

time of my fieldwork (1980–1988), really put into practice, contrary to the situation in the HIH.

In Afghanistan, the conception of an elite party did not survive the Communist coup of 1978, except for the Hizb-i Islami led by Hekmatyar. The necessity to organize the massive peasant uprisings led to the creation of "mass parties," where the screening of new members was minimal, if it was done at all.

The State: A Shared Model Among Islamists. State and society are conceived on the same model as the party, which prefigures, in a *jâhiliyya* society, what should become a true Islamic society. Just as with an ideal party structure, the future Islamic society should consist of a consensus of faithful members; a *shura*, or advisory council; and a strong leadership with both political and religious qualifications, the leader being called amir or caliph. The party is thus a model for a true Islamic society.

Sovereignty is with God, not the people. Neither state nor people can be a source of the law. In this sense, democracy is not Islamic, because the people cannot change or evade God's law. This conception of sovereignty also devalues the state.[12] "The state according to Islam is nothing more than a combination of men working together as servants of God to carry out His will and purposes," wrote Maududi.[13] Yet, at the same time, Maududi advocates the establishment of a constitution, and Rabbani observed in an editorial entitled "Why Are We Not 'democratic'?": "For some people democracy might mean 'government of the people, by the people, for the people' with attribution of sovereignty to the people . . . Islam will be against such a democracy."[14] Thus the declaration about sovereignty being with God alone seems to be more a theological principle than the basis for a practical political program.

Leaders and Political Actors. At the head of the party, and eventually of the state, is the amir, assisted by an advisory council, or shura. The term amir is used by contemporary Islamists (including Arabs) as the equivalent of a "right" political leader, the one

12. Qutb, in Carré, *Mystique*, p. 177.
13. Kalim Bahadur, *The Jama'at-i Islami of Pakistan*, p. 161.
14. *The Mirror of Jihâd* (March–April 1982), pp. 3 and 6.

who heads the Islamic party. Islamists gave up the idea of a caliph, the political and religious leader of the whole umma, because for them the Islamic revolution should be implemented, *hic et nunc*, in the framework of the existing nation-states without waiting for the reconstitution of the umma; the latter should follow, not precede, the implementation of an Islamic revolution in various countries. The amir is more than a mere political leader; he has a religious legitimation. How is the amir designated and who are the members of the shura? All Islamist political literature stresses that the amir should be the "best" Muslim, not a de facto ruler. More broadly, the question is how to define, in the Islamist political vision, a political "actor." If the present rulers are purely de facto rulers and lack legitimacy, and if the ulama are disqualified because of their casuistic manipulation of the shari'a and their compromising with an illegitimate state, then who is qualified to lead first the "Islamic party" and then the "Islamic society"? The question of leadership is the cornerstone of Islamist ideology.

It is now largely accepted that the Islamist movement is composed of urban laymen, generally educated in Westernized government schools (such professions as education, engineering, medicine),[15] who have seldom pursued theological studies. The problem for them is how to claim religious legitimacy against the ulama. Islamists advocate a reopening of the "door of interpretation," or *ijtihâd* (personal interpretation of the religious law), which would allow them to give their own interpretation of the Qur'ān and the Sunna. In this manner, they would break the religious monopoly of the mullahs. This demand is more or less openly made. For example, JIA statutes encourage its members to think for themselves and become *ahl-i tahqîq* or *mohaqîq* ("of those who are seeking truth"); the statutes also equally attribute to the ulama and mohaqîq the right to ijtihâd,[16] thus indicating

15. On the social background of the Islamists, see Dekmejian, *Islam in Revolution*; Kepel and Yann (eds.), *Intellectuels et militants*; and Olivier Roy, *Islam and Resistance*, chap. 4.

16. *Osûl-e Ba'yat*, p. 8: "The ijtihâdât of the ulama and of the researchers [*mohaqeqîn*] must be done in order to please God." The term mohaqeqîn is vague enough to include intellectuals.

that ulama and mohaqîq are in fact two different categories. Even if not explicitly stated, it is obvious that mohaqîq denotes any lay Islamist intellectual.

The right to ijtihâd is admitted by Maududi and Qutb,[17] as it was by the Salafis. For Qutb, it takes the meaning of avoiding *taqlid* (blind imitation) rather than of innovating.[18] The problem is that by emphasizing ijtihâd, one may bypass the shari'a and undermine the very foundations of an Islamic society. The question of ijtihâd is thus linked to the existence of a leadership. But a problem arises because, for Sunni Islamists, there is no "obvious" leader, as there is among the Shi'a (the *marja'i taqlîd*, or "source of imitation," i.e., the designation given to the small group of Grand Ayatollahs). Moreover, the lay background of the Islamists has led them on occasion to claim the right for a noncleric to become the amir or guide. Hence, the alternative: Either the amir, cleric or not, necessarily has the right to ijtihâd as an amir, even if such a claim degrades religious studies, which is inconsistent with the claim that the shari'a should be the foundation of society; or the amir should be the most learned of the ulama. The latter fits neither with the social composition of the Islamist movement and its anti-ulama bias nor with its will to reopen the door of ijtihâd. On this key question, the cleavage between fundamentalists and Islamists is obvious and critical. For example, the Afghan Hizb-i Islami's statutes mention that the party leader is not necessarily an *'alim* (Hekmatyar is a former student of engineering). He should, however, be seen as a spiritual leader[19] with the right to ijtihâd, even concerning the everyday life of the members.[20] Yet, the party's statutes never state that the amir

17. For Maududi, see Kalim Bahadur, *The Jama'at-i Islami*, pp. 165, 207. The right to ijtihâd depends on religious knowledge.

18. See Carré, *Mystique*, p. 70.

19. See *Mas'uliat*, p. 85: The leader must be considered by the member *shekl-e yek pîshvâ'y-yi rûhânî*, "like a spiritual director."

20. "Is the member ready to acknowledge that his opinion is wrong if it contradicts the decisions [*faysala*] of the leader [*maqâmât-i rahbarî*] about the problems of interpretations [*masâ'il-i ijtihâdî*] concerning the daily events?" The answer is obviously that he should be ready. *Mas'uliat*, pp. 85, 87.

should be a religious scholar. Complete loyalty to the amir tends to replace personal ijtihâd, resulting in what is more nearly a Shi'ite attitude, a paradoxical position for Sunni Hanbalis. Followers, and eventually the whole umma, should swear obedience to the amir through the *bay'a* (oath of allegiance). The only limitation to his power is that he must seek advice through a council (shura).

Moderate Islamists agree that the amir is not necessarily a cleric, but, if he is not, they tend to reduce his right to ijtihâd.[21] They agree on bay'a and shura, but for them the bay'a is more a contract than an oath of allegiance, and the council (shura) has the power to replace and criticize the amir.

For both moderate and radical Islamists, the shura should appoint the amir, whatever his powers. But the shura is not a parliament that can make law, because sovereignty (and lawmaking) is solely at the hands of God. Therefore, the shura is a consulting and advising body for the amir, in accord with numerous Qur'ānic verses that encourage the ruler to seek advice. Here arise two problems: Who are the members of the shura, and what is the need for a shura if its advice is not binding?

Islamists used to refer to the *ahl al-hall wa al-'aqd*, "those able to bind and loose," according to a Qur'ānic sura. But who are they? The ulama? Or anyone whose knowledge entitles him to practice ijtihâd? Or the entire umma? The implications are obvious. If only the ulama are permitted to be members of the shura, that entails the creation of a clerical state. If it is the educated, in a broader sense, who are entitled to exercise ijtihâd, the lay Islamist intellectuals have their day. If it is the umma, general elections are justified, and then an Islamic society becomes compatible with a parliamentary system (as in Iran). Islamists of course include themselves (intellectuals with little religious

---

21. Al-Hâshimi envisages both cases: an amir being from *ahl-i ijtihâd*, from those who have the right to ijtihâd, and an amir who is not, and therefore should obligatorily be assisted by a shura (*Misâq*, p. 38). The fact that this text is quoted by a JIA journal shows the reluctance of moderate Islamists to give too much power to the amir or caliph. In this case, Maududi also stresses the limitations of the amir's powers (*Jihâd in Islâm*, p. 30).

knowledge) in the *ahl al-hall wa al-'aqd*.[22] One way to avoid the opposition between ulama and intellectuals is to give the latter a religious education; the HIH makes it mandatory for members of its Central Council to acquire such religious knowledge, implicitly assuming that most of them have not had such knowledge.[23] To consult the shura is not binding on the ruler, but it is assumed that a good Muslim should. The shura principle might thus justify different theories. For instance, the HIH shifted, in its political programs, from advocating the constitution of a consultative assembly (shura) whose membership is drawn from the *ahl al-hall wa al-'aqd* to calling, in 1988, for general elections without conditions of participation (except for the exclusion of women).[24]

The question of who can be a member of the shura, and who should elect its members, thus remains open. Even Sayyid Qutb does not provide a blueprint.

The only principle on which fundamentalists and Islamists agree—that is, implementation of shari'a—has never been developed into a political ideology. It is, rather, a mere motto. The reason is probably that the shari'a belongs to the ulama, and Islamist intellectuals are careful not to be explicit about it. The second reason is that the Islamists' main contribution to the question of the Islamic state concerns areas about which the shari'a has nothing to say.

The Uncertainties of the Islamic State: Virtue as the Only Guide. Despite their considerable differences, the views of the ulama and the Islamists agree on one principle. A truly Islamic society is based on the virtue of its members. Preaching, enforcement of the shari'a, and striving for personal moral improvement are the real issues in an Islamic society—more than building institutions

22. Carré, *Mystique*, p. 206.

23. *Mas'uliat*, p. 99.

24. In the booklet *Clues to the Solution of the Afghan Crisis*, Hekmatyar went so far as to criticize the theory of *ahl al-hall wa al-'aqd*, showing convincingly that it is not consistent. Instead, he advocated general elections. This is one instance in which the line adopted by a radical Islamist breaks with the usual political conception of Islam, whether fundamentalist or Islamist, and adopts instead a purely secular approach.

or political parties. The weakness of political Islam is in this inability to think in terms of "polity." The famous affirmation that *din* and *siyasa* (religion and politics) are a single entity in fact implies a secondary role for siyasa. Politics is conducted outside any conceptual framework.

But what kind of "virtue" are we speaking of? If we take the example of HIH's "members' duties," the party's hierarchical levels correspond to fixed levels of virtues (taqwa): Ordinary members, members of the council, and the amir are all defined by their ethical nature. Article 11 states that a member should be a "good" Muslim. That is followed by recommendations about devotions, daily life, ethical conduct ("modesty, abnegation, no slandering"). A member's discipline within the party and his total obedience to the amir are seen as a way to purify himself by degrees, according to the Sufi way. The member should attract outsiders to the party, because he is himself an ethical model (*Mas'uliat*, page 79). But he has himself a model in mind: the amir, who is like a "father..., a teacher..., a spiritual leader ... and a political leader" (page 85). Any candidate for party membership is required to study the biography of party leaders (page 86) and totally accept the guidelines given by the leadership. He should accept the ijtihâd of the leader on questions concerning daily life even if it is contrary to his own opinion (p. 87).

"The members of the Central Council should endeavor to exemplify the most perfect model of Islamic virtues, in order to preserve the unity of views and action" (page 103.) Unity of the party is based on personal virtue. "The moral and spiritual superiority of the members of the Central Council, in comparison with the other members of the party, should be absolutely clear and evident" (page 104).

At the highest level, there is a list (page 105) of virtues the amir should embody in addition to those incumbent upon the members of the Central Council. He should "embody in his own acting personality the principles, bases and foundations [*osûl wa moqrarât*] of the party, and in his leadership observe the *hudûd*, the mandatory and supererogatory precepts [*ahkâm*] of the shari'a." (Interestingly enough, the party here comes before God.) The amir should abstain from sin and whatever is forbidden (*munkar*); he should embody *sadaqât* (sincerity), *insâf* (equity), *'adâlat* (justice), *ikhlâs* (purity), and "surpass every member of the society in the qualities that are required in the personality of a believer."

His followers must swear an oath of allegiance (*bay'a*) (page 26), which can be broken only if the amir transgresses the shari'a. In fact, because the amir is supposed to be the best Muslim, once chosen, he holds considerable power, limited only by the shari'a. The limit of the amir's power is his own virtue, if we except the emergency situation where he can be deposed by the shura. But who can judge the virtue of the amir? The amir is supposed to know better than other people. There is no political body that can interpret the shari'a better than he. Thus the paradox is that the amir is limited by a law of which he is the best interpreter. He is thus supposed to be the best limitation to his own power. Once more, personal virtue is the necessary condition of the good working of the political system.

The corresponding guidebook of the Jam'iyyat-i Islami is oriented toward religiosity but makes it also obvious that personal piety is a prerequisite to establishing an Islamic order. A member should first know Islam, the Qur'ān, and the Sunna. The duties of the member are listed as follows:

1) Reform of the self (*islâh-i nafs*);
2) Reform of the family;
3) Reform of society;
4) Reform of state power (*hukumat*).

Little ranking is made among members, who are responsible before God, not the amir (*Osûl-e Ba'yat*, page 23), and who should think for themselves (page 30). The contradiction between the call for an Islamic society and the possibility of appointing a lay amir with little religious knowledge has driven JIA into a direction opposite that of the HIH. Instead of stressing the charismatic nature of the amir, thus elevating him above the ulama, JIA underplays the role of the amir and, consequently, of the party itself. The main duties (*da'wa*, or preaching jihad) are personal, not collective, duties (page 16); the party is a means, not an end. There is little about discipline; the member is asked to regard the amir as a "father" and a political, but not a religious, leader (page 24). The text stresses confidence (*i'timâd*) more than obedience (*iti'ât*). The Prophet alone is called the "guide." The expression *kadr-e rahbar* (chief executive) is preferred to that of amir (page 23ff).

The JIA guidebook reiterates the Muslim credo (oneness of God) and condemns the cult of saints and of the dead (Article 12). These details can be understood only in the light of present polemics against both Wahhabism and Shi'ism. Recognition of all Sunni Imams (Article 6 of its statutes) is a way to take some distance from the Hanbali bias, so frequent among Sunni Islamists. Moreover, the fact that jokes are permitted (page 39) is an implicit criticism of the Wahhabis. The repeated motto "The Qur'ān is our constitution and the Holy Prophet (Praise Be Upon Him) is our leader and guide [*rahbar*]" (page 13) is implicit criticism of the Iranian Revolution (Muḥammad as rahbar vs. Khumayni as rahbar). JIA has been careful to distance itself from the Iranian Revolution, first because, being mostly Persian-speaking, it has had tens of thousands of followers among Afghans living in Iran; secondly, because it is closer to the mainstream of the Egyptian Muslim Brothers (as represented by Shaykh Talmasani), it is thus critical of radicals.

The uncertainty of the Islamist blueprint is that while claiming to establish political Islam, it conceptually ignores institutions, sociology, and history. Institutions are nothing without the virtue and the faith of the men who are in charge of them. But where are to be found political institutions that work only if people are virtuous, and what is the need for political institutions if the people are virtuous? Every political appointment is qualified by a set of virtues and responsibilities (*mas'uliyat*), which should be embodied in the appointee. For instance, JIA's *Osûl-e Bay'at* states that the administration should be honest, close to the people and good to them, should act with justice and equity, ensure security, morality, etc. Such a list shows that administration is not seen as a system but as the expression of the virtues of its civil servants.[25] In HIH's *Mas'uliat*, divergences between mem-

25. Paragraph entitled "On the Specifics of an Islamic Government," *Osûl-e Ba'yat*, p. 18.

bers are nothing more than "misunderstandings (*su' tafâhum*)."[26]
Thus, "policy" and "politics" are replaced, and nullified, by ethics.

Because nothing worthwhile happened since the Golden Age
of the Prophet and the time of the Four Rightly Guided Caliphs,
history is only a stock of paradigms and anecdotes. Whereas
sociology conceives of societal divisions and differences as facts,
not as defects, for the Islamists this amounts to introducing *fitna*
(division of the community). Fitna is seen as a sin, not a sociological fact. Thus fitna stems either from a lack of religious faith or
is the result of a conspiracy.

This does not mean that the political thinking of Islamists
ignores institutions, history, or sociology. For example, any mujahidin field commander knows about tribal segmentation and
how to deal with it. But he does not integrate this knowledge
into his Islamic political framework. Hence, the striking opposition between political speeches and programs and the actual practice of everyday politics, which fact contributes to undermining
the validity of Islamist political references.[27] The reason for this
discrepancy is that social segmentation, whatever its basis (tribal,
ethnic, or economic), is attributed to a lack of Islam, not to an
essential characteristic of any human society. For instance, Qâzi
Amin, former deputy of Hekmatyar, acknowledged that Afghan
society is made up of "different races, languages, groups, and
various sects [*mazhab*] and tribes [*qawm*]," but only Islam could
unite such a society and create an "Islamic order" (*nizam-i Islami*),
which cannot be "semi-Islamic" (*shabhi-Islami*). One has "to Islamize the life of the people of Afghanistan" (*"Islamize kardan"*)—a
strange neologism—in order to surmount such intrinsic segmentation.[28]

26. *Mas'uliat*, p. 110.
27. A striking fact, borne out by field research in Afghanistan, is that
Islamist commanders are reluctant to give the researcher information about
tribal links, ethnic affiliation, and familial backgrounds, while traditional
tribal leaders are, on the contrary, proud to show their knowledge about
genealogy and tribal affiliations.
28. Qâzi Amin Wâqed, "Hukumat-e Ayande-ye Afghanistan."

In fact, as acknowledged by the editors of *Afghan News* (*Jamiat-i Islami*, 15 October 1987, page 1), "Islam does not offer a blueprint of an Islamic government." One cannot find in contemporary Sunni thinking an "Islamic constitution," in contrast with the Iranian experience. For the Sunni, there is no need to draft a precise political model, because if society becomes Islamic, there will be no need for such a model: "The Holy Qur'ān is our Constitution." One thus comes full circle. One has to create an Islamic society in order to enable people to achieve their religious ideals, but such a society can work only if the people have already reached a state of personal perfection. If the shari'a is implemented, then people will be just and happiness will come (*Misâq-i khûn*, no. 19, 1987). There is the quandary. To have an Islamic society you need good Muslims, and to have good Muslims (except in small communities), you need an Islamic society. The only way to break out of this circle would be to have an amir who would be *index sui*, that is, able to demonstrate his nature by his acts. Hence, there develops the search for a charismatic leader and the inability to think of politics in terms of a constitution and specific institutions. Muhammad was the last Prophet, and there is no Hidden Imam in Sunni political thought.

CHAPTER FOUR

JIHAD
AS AN
ETHICAL MODEL

THE MUJAHIDIN MODEL OF WAR, the jihad, is supposed to differ from both guerrilla and conventional warfare in the sense that it is an ethical model and a religious duty, not a particular concept of tactics and strategy. But as we shall see, the lack of practical military thinking among mujahidin (with the exception of Ahmed Shah Massoud) has led to a return to traditional warfare aimed at restoring the balance of power, not at destroying the enemy.

Traditional Warfare

Traditional Afghani warfare has been observed and studied by sociologists and British military officers mainly among Pashtun tribes.[1] Ghilzays and eastern Pashtuns have a tradition of unruliness and violence not matched by the other ethnic groups until the Soviet invasion of December 1979. But in nontribalized areas, patterns of traditional warfare seem to be the same as in tribal areas, with a lesser degree of violence. Up to the present, traditional Afghan warfare has aimed at either opposing segmentary groups against each other or opposing a coalition of these segmentary groups (at the tribal level) against the state. Such traditional warfare is unacquainted with the notion of total war and thus seems not to be adapted to modern warfare. Its main patterns are as follows:

1) There is no clear-cut separation between peace and war. All social relationships are ruled by a code of hostility, compen-

1. Akbar Ahmed, *Millennium and Charisma Among Sawt Pathans*; idem, *Pushtun Economy and Society*; Louis Dupree, "Tribal Warfare in Afghanistan and Pakistan"; Leon Poullada, *Reform and Rebellion in Afghanistan*; see also numerous British books and reports on the Afghan wars from 1840 to 1919.

63

sated by a code of hospitality, all the more strict because the insecurity seems permanent. In Pashtun areas, the sense of insecurity is constant (people used to live in fortified farms, or *qala*), because vendettas can break out at any time and at any level of the social scale (from two cousins competing for a bride, to a whole clan dividing itself into two opposing groups). Thus, the difference between a personal vendetta and an intertribal conflict is simply in the number of people involved. The fighting group is the civil society, with the same leadership and no professionalization of fighters.

2) Military encounters are limited in time and space and affect everyday life only slightly. They usually occur outside villages; purdah (seclusion of women) and privacy are usually respected. Business goes on as usual in markets and bazaars. Fighting ceases during harvest or other specific occasions. Moreover, fighting generally does not transcend the "solidarity space" that is the territory where a group (a qawm) feels at home. This space is not a homogeneous territory in terms of inhabitants but must be conceived as a network of friends and foes. For anyone wandering out of this space, there is a clear sense of insecurity. A breakthrough outside this space is exceptional and of short duration. It usually occurs only if there is a call for jihad.

3) The objective is not to destroy the adversary, but to improve one's relative standing vis-à-vis other qawms and to establish new social equilibrium. Combat is more symbolic than real: The goal is limited to the spoils, as an end in itself or as a punishment to be inflicted on the adversary; its aim is not conquest of territory or destruction of a group. Raids for cattle, assassination, and ambushes are the usual tactics and imply mobility and surprise. Open fighting, by contrast, is static and demonstrative, a show of force that may lead the parties to compromise. Two groups fire at each other from their *sangar* (barricades), or at the government post, without trying any surprise maneuver. Fighting is always combined with negotiation. Specific groups are used to act as peace brokers—mullahs, *myân*, *sayyad*, *rish-e safid* ("white beards"), the state, or even a foreign power. What is at stake is

the search for prestige in the form of economic advantages taken from the opponents, including land or spoils, "blood money," or even state allowances (given in order to keep a group at peace). The notion of equilibrium and status quo is a constant in the tribal vision of violence and war.

4) Traditional warfare is a domestic competition between equals; values at stake are precedence, pride and honor (*gheyrat* and *nâmus*). The tension is permanent between the myth of consensus (tribal *jirqah*; Muslim *umma*) and the violence of the relationship between equals, not so much for leadership in the political sense of the term as for precedence. The important issue is "Who is the bigger man?" (*kalan nafar*). The concept of khan is nothing more than the preservation of such a precedence embodied in a man, who can be challenged at almost any time by a rival. Both the foreigner and the subordinate are in a safer position than the native and the peer. In fact, traditional warfare is linked to the question of leadership.

Precisely because it happens behind closed doors, tribal war is neither ideological nor political; the state being outside the tribal space, one will not hesitate to make an alliance with the state against a rival. The state is not denied but is made instrumental to achieve one's local aims. As long as the state does not appear to be willing to change the rules of the game (for example, by trying to build a road, establish an army post, or a local administration), it is accepted. Even in such cases, however, the techniques of combat against the state will be similar to those used in the war among clans, but it will be merely demonstrative: A tribal group will besiege or stage an attack against a military outpost, but without trying to take it. In fact, contrary to the cliché that makes state and tribes antagonists, tribes, however rebellious they may be, need a state, but not too strong a state, to act as a referee, to maintain intramural conflicts at a low level, to avoid the creation of a vacuum that could pit them against each other outside their "solidarity space," and simply to protect business. Smugglers need borders, thieves need trade, highway robbers need highways—tribes need the state.

The Jihad Model

At regular intervals during Afghan history, a call to fight a jihad against infidels, heretics, or unbelievers has led to a *levée en masse* of the people, bypassing the traditional segmentation and bringing tribal levies outside their "solidarity space," usually under the banner of religious leaders.

Sociology of Jihad. Compared with traditional warfare, jihad entails radical change. It is called by a religious figure who is usually alien to the tribe; it does not happen behind closed doors, but opposes interior (the Muslim umma) to exterior (*kafir*: heretics or unbelievers); it transcends tribal segmentation by referring to the umma; it transcends tribal codes and values by referring to Islam and to shari'a. Symmetry and equilibrium, those obsessions of tribes, are no longer applicable.

Jihad provides an opportunity for new leaders to supplant traditional tribal leadership. For a century, in Afghanistan, jihad leaders have been religious figures.[2] But as we have seen, the war against the Soviets enabled the Islamists to participate. The instrument of their breakthrough has been the political parties, a notion foreign to the traditional jihad. From the beginning, the parties, being based on ideological commitments, have been seen as nonpartisan in terms of ethnic and tribal identity.

Jihad as a Political Model. "The purpose of Jehad is . . . to establish the supremacy of God's word . . . to eliminate the oppression which is imposed on Muslims . . . to establish a righteous and just society and to preserve it," states a JIA editorial.[3] Jihad introduces new criteria of legitimation. The jihad space is neither that of the solidarity group nor of the nation-state, but of the whole umma. In this symbolic space, one circulates upwards toward victory or downwards toward the hijra; the Afghan refugees in Peshawar understood their exile as a religious duty as much as a search for safety. Jihad implies peace and unity

---

2. For the 1920s, see Poullada, *Reform and Rebellion.*
3. *The Mirror of Jihâd*, May-June 1982, editorial ("What Is Jehad and Who is a Mujahid?"), p. 9.

among Muslims; hence the negation of tribal and ethnic segmentation; local conflicts among mujahidin are interpreted in terms of "misunderstandings," which should be managed through mediation and truce.

But the denial of segmentation among Muslims does not mean that jihad can provide a model of the state. Jihad ignores the concept of the state, or, more accurately, the state (*dawlat*) is seen as purely instrumental and is often identified with individual leaders. It defends the nation (*milla*), which is seen as the community of the faithful surrounded by infidels (*kuffâr*).[4] This instrumental vision of the state is consistent with the fundamentalist conception of the state, as a mere tool to implement the shari'a.

Jihad as Warfare. The objective of jihad is to topple an existing infidel power or to crush invading forces. The instrument is an army of mujahidin. The resistance against the Communist coup of 1978 and *a fortiori* against the Soviet invasion was done in the name of jihad.

How has this shaped the Afghan mujahidin movement? In fact, if the strategy of jihad differs from traditional warfare, and the number of people involved is far higher, the tactics of the jihad are nevertheless those of traditional Afghani warfare—discontinuity, displays of military might instead of attempts to annihilate the enemy, a tendency for plundering, plus rivalries among khans, tribes, or ethnic groups, which reappear whenever victory seems near and which usually manage to forestall the expected victory. Thus, what should become military victories are not exploited, and the ulama can only impose shari'a and discipline for a short period of time. The jihad does not know the ABCs of war according to Clausewitz.

4. Historically speaking, Afghanistan refers to the land of the Afghans, that is, the Pashtun. Nobody inside Afghanistan will call himself Afghan if he is not a Pashtun. This does not mean that there is no sense of a shared identity; but this identity is based mainly on religion: Afghanistan, as a *milla*, or nation, is seen by most "Afghans" as the tract of territory that has been preserved from foreign (British and Russian) colonialism or "heretic" (that is, Iranian Shi'ism) control. That is why Afghan identity is barely separable from Sunni Hanafi identity, hence the suspicion towards the Shi'a.

Jihad as an Ethical Model. Although jihad provides neither a political nor a military model, it does offer an ethical one. Jihad is a moral duty, a personal religious achievement. Achieving a worldly goal is not the primary obligation for jihad, since jihad is a relationship between the believer and God, not between the believer and the infidel.[5] It is an act of faith. "The aim of the endeavors and efforts of a Muslim mujahid in the oath and action of his personal jihad and combat is only to please God."[6] "The purpose of jihad is . . . to purify oneself morally and spiritually."[7] Hence the demonstrative nature of the fighting, the individualism of the mujahid, his rejection of an overly strict discipline. The mujahid is often a part-time warrior. Here, traditional warfare fits with the religious perception of war as an act of worship.

Jihad is aimed at infidels (and, in this case of Afghanis, it was aimed at the Soviets), and preserves intact the hierarchies and rivalries on the Muslim side, although it does favor the use of Islamic parties to achieve its goals. In fact, a rank and file mujahid has two levels of reference: the jihad as far as the enemy is concerned, plus the traditional segmentation as far as his fellow mujahidin are concerned.

The Afghan Mujahid: Between Tribal Warrior and Modern Guerrilla

There is nothing in either traditional warfare or jihad that could push the mujahidin toward a modern, Clausewitzian warfare, except models introduced from above by party leaders. The refusal of military professionalism is particularly striking. It is a constant in Muslim history that the professional soldier (*askar*) is usually despised in comparison to the mujahid, volunteer and believer, but also to the warrior and even to the tradesman and craftsman.[8] The askar is viewed as a mercenary (*mazdur*, or wage-earner), either the victim of a forced conscription or too ignorant

5. Jean Paul Charnay, *L'Islam et la guerre.*
6. *Osûl-e Bay'at*, p. 13.
7. *The Mirror of Jihâd*, May-June 1982.
8. See Charnay, *L'Islam*, p. 252.

to have been able to follow another profession. Regarded as irresponsible, he will not be executed if he is captured (except by the more radical groups) but lectured to and released (which is not the case for the officer). One of the most striking characteristics of the Afghan resistance is its refusal of military professionalism, except in the areas controlled by Massoud. The absence of a structured chain of command, of tiers of officers between the chief and the troops (except the "head of group," which corresponds to a sergeant), of tactical training, and of specialization in military operations are negative consequences of this rejection of a military model. The chief is in charge of everything, from the direction of the battle to the nomination of sentries.

The fact that the mujahid remains first of all a civilian links him to his qawm and its territory or networks. A mujahidin group has no mobility outside its territory, except to reach Pakistan and bring back weapons, at its own risk. The group will be taxed at best, at worst plundered by other mujahidin groups, sometimes even belonging to the same party. A mujahidin armed group seeking to wage a battle against a specific target (military post) has to negotiate with the local population the "right" to attack. A refusal to do so might lead to a temporary alliance of the local population and mujahidin groups with the government against "intruders."

This rejection of militarization distinguishes the Afghan resistance from other liberation movements. Although the population of Afghan refugees is the largest in the world, there is no external army such as the Algerian FLN or the PLO. This is not only due to the reluctance of the Pakistani government to permit such an intrusion but also to the refusal by the resistance to create a state apparatus in the refugee camps. The rejection of the military is linked to the rejection of the state.

What remains of jihad in these conditions? An ethical model. The military results matter less than the personal moral achievement of the mujahid. Acts of personal bravery are committed individually, without regard to collective action. The model is the martyr, the *shahid*. To be killed is the real victory.[9] There

---

9. *Osûl-e Ba'yat*, p. 22.

is a "shahid culture."[10] The jihad provides a culture, not a strategy. That makes for military inefficiency, which could also lapse into mere show and demonstration, reverting to a pattern common in traditional Afghani warfare.[11]

Most local resistance commanders tried of their own free will to avoid any professionalization or militarization that might threaten traditional society's structures. On the contrary, they endeavored to translate into traditional terms new elements introduced by modern warfare. Not only combat tactics, as we have seen, but also arms distribution, taxation, dispensing of justice, and logistical organization were carried out according to traditional models. There was no, or little, organization of passive defense, enlistment of civilians, or creation of an administration. Let us cite two typical examples: women and the economy. There were no women fighters. Respect for the harem and purdah (keeping women in secluded quarters) was a part of what Afghans were preserving against the Soviets. Including women in combat would have been a denial of the very reason for the combat. Modernization of society as a result of the war reached its limit here. Women were part of the private sphere of life. The private economy operated without much interference on the part of the mujahidin, who drew upon it both for logistics and for supplies. There was no "mujahidin economy."

The strategic and cultural immobility of the jihad is well pictured in the role played by the Afghani concept of "military base" (*markaz*): This was a mujahidin camp protected by antiaircraft defense and heavy weapons. No families were ever seen there, and the mujahidin organized themselves for daily life: bakers, gardeners, stable boys, waiters, etc. The markaz did not exist in

10. P. Centlivres, "Les tulipes rouges d'Afghanistan."

11. Media coverage of the Afghan War is used to stress what looked like modern military action, with much gunfire and smoke. But the accuracy, or even reality, of such coverage has to be questioned. Such coverage is often either faked or at least overemphasized. That is perhaps because routine fighting and individual acts of bravery are difficult to cover by a TV crew or are simply not interesting enough for them. It does not mean that such deeds do not take place.

traditional Afghani tribal warfare, since between operations the soldier lived at home. From the markaz, mobile groups set forth to patrol the solidarity space and keep track of any government presence. The enemy garrison might be kept for years under passive siege, the roads ambushed at intervals. The solidarity space thus recentered around the markaz and visited by mobile groups of soldiers was called the "front" (*jabha*).

There are two markaz traditions in Muslim history: the retreat of the bandit of honor and the *ribat* (fortified monasteries) of the military brotherhoods on the frontiers of the Muslim world.[12] In Afghanistan, a few markaz are found at the "banditry" frontiers, such as that of Amir Rassoul, in Baghlan, where perched on a mountaintop it serves mainly to levy taxes on the countryside below. Even among the true mujahidin, however, the "base" is less an element of military strategy than a sociopolitical restructuring of space. It is a matter of reconstituting a solidarity group (qawm) around a chief drawn from the new elite acting like a traditional khan, even if he is of quite modest origin. He keeps a guest table, distributes ammunition, money, and small gifts. The social reclassification brought about by the war in no way implies abandoning the traditional concept of authority. Those newly promoted adopt the way of life and conduct of the former notables (significantly, the title khan is tacked on to the name of commanders who were formerly students with no prestige but who came to command broad military fronts—Basir Khan, Ismail Khan, Bashir Khan. . . .). The sociology of being a chief has changed with respect to the past but not the behavior of the one who is perceived as the new khan. The chief is above all the one who *gives*; arms and ammunition have replaced money and food.

The analysis we have made explains the unexpected change in the war in Afghanistan after the Soviet departure in February 1989. The mujahidin failed in the transition from a guerrilla war to a conventional war less because of military factors than because such a transition presupposes the abandonment of traditional

12. See Charnay, *L'Islam*, pp. 232, 250.

forms of warfare and the imposition of state patterns among the guerrillas—that is, the introduction of a centralized command and the mobilization of combat units without considering the ethnic, tribal, and qawm division of an area. The Pakistani soldiers who pressed the guerrillas to join the conventional war in 1989 looked on Afghanistan as a "headquarters operations map" upon which one moves little blue, red, and green flags over a space where units are interchangeable and objectives quantifiable. As seen by Afghans, however, this was a sociocultural space: that of tribes, ethnic groups, zones of influence of one chief or another.

The Massoud Model: A Compromise Between Jihad and Modern War

When one examines the several hundred Afghan mujahidin "commands" inside the country, one finds that all use the traditional model of warfare. Only one, however, established not only a modern army, but, more particularly, a modern strategy. This was the Massoud command.

At first, the Massoud front, located in northeast Afghanistan, followed the typical qawm structure. Massoud, a militant Islamist and former engineering student, took possession of the lower valley of Panjshir, where he was born, and conquered it with a handful of Jam'iyyat-i Islami party members who arrived from Peshawar during the winter of 1979–80. The local people joined the Jam'iyyat because its head, Rabbani, was a Persian-speaking Sunni like themselves, because it was the first party to take up arms, and because the valley had an old tradition of fundamentalist opposition, transmitted by a network of traditionalist ulama. The inhabitants of the adjacent valleys (Shotol, Hazara) as well as those higher up (Paryan) immediately joined, although they did not identify themselves as Panjshiris.

From the outset, there was a broadening of the solidarity space. Massoud's basic outfit was composed of Panjshiris educated or working in Kabul, thus less subjected to the duties of the qawm. The people of Panjshir were of course peasants, but they had long been accustomed to emigrate to Kabul, where they formed a large proportion of transport workers, mechanics, and cooks in the households of foreigners. In this community of "emigrant" Panjshiris, a regional Panjshiri identity arose, transcending membership in the village qawms. For these, the qawm is Panjshiri, no longer *Nuruz Kheyl* (name of Massoud's family, said to have come from Central Asia) or Sayyid or other possible rubric. Massoud's two trumps were thus the control of a homogeneous solidarity space (without tribal or other subdivisions) and control of urbanized and technically competent personnel, while nevertheless retaining a link with traditional society. Soon after eliminating a few Maoist and "Hizbi" (of Hekmatyar's party) pockets, Massoud reigned in the name of Jam'iyyat over all Panjshiris, making possible his first victory, in the spring of 1980, over Soviet and government forces. To this point, no new ground had been broken.

From that moment on, Massoud played a part in the introduction of an innovative military model long before there was a question of abandoning the solidarity space. The Massoud model consisted in militarizing his troops and turning them into professional soldiers. The military apparatus was no longer merely an armed duplicate of civil society, at least insofar as one rose in the hierarchy. This was in fact the model of Vietnam's General Giap. First, one found a base (*qarargah*) where a locally recruited group (*grup-e mahalli*) of nonspecialists ensured public order and self-defense within a few villages; these nonspecialists used to rotate in performing productive community tasks. Then, at the district level, an "assault group" (*grup-e zarbati*) organized local, but permanent, soldiers and provided them with uniforms and heavy weapons (antitank guns and machine guns). This group participated only in operations conducted within the district and constituted the first line of defense in case of a surprise enemy attack. Thus far, we are still within the traditional solidarity space.

Then came the "mobile group" (*motaharek*), recruited and based locally but moving beyond the borders of the solidarity space for strictly military purposes. This was the first example of operations outside the solidarity space. Beginning in 1985,

"central units" appeared whose recruitment was totally independent of a qawm network. These elite units served as a training
ground for cadres of a future army. Any military operation against
a post entailed the participation of central units, mobile groups,
and local groups. Beginning in the fall of 1986, Massoud launched
a series of such attacks against government bases held by battalion-
size garrisons—those of Nahrin, Farkhar, Kalafgan, Keshm, and
Koranomunjan. Then, finally, in August 1988, Taloqan, the first
provincial capital, fell into Massoud's hands. These operations
took place in four different provinces.

The essential problem thus was to transcend the Panjshiri
solidarity space and integrate other solidarity spaces so as to move
toward a "national" space conceived in strategic terms. What
Massoud did was to attract local non-Panjshiri commanders, dis-
affected with their traditional qawm leaders, convincing them of
the superiority of his model and, after they were trained, sending
them back to their native zones, where they developed his model
with Panjshiri advisers. Belonging generally to that same urbanized, educated generation, these new commanders found social
advancement by entering the ranks of Massoud's group; this move
enabled them to evade local hierarchies that had become too
onerous for them. By manipulating a sociological mutation—the
rise of educated persons outside the powerful kinship networks—
Massoud could aspire to force a military (and therefore political)
change. The peasantry followed to the extent that joining Massoud's ranks enabled them to escape petty warlords. By 1982,
groups who considered themselves ethnically different from the
Panjshiris were calling themselves members of the Panjshiri
qawm, such as the Sunnis of the Hazara Valley, or the people of
Shotol, who even spoke a different language (*Parachi*).

At the village level, Massoud left traditional structures absolutely untouched. His model was imposed from above through
the military. To give it physical expression, in 1985 he created
the Northern Supervisory Council (*shura-ye nazar*), a collective
structure intended to go beyond segmented solidarity spaces by
employing the political cadre of the Jam'iyyat Party (although a

number of party officials remained reticent toward a structure that denied them the new status of khan: that is, a traditional notable who acquired his title by means of war). District governors were appointed by the council and, insofar as possible, from outside local qawms. Cultural, public health, finance, and legal commissions formed embryos of future ministries. Beyond the military organization, a model of government structure was taking shape, superposed over the traditional notables and the qawm system without, however, supplanting them, for any attempt to eliminate the traditional system would have thrown part of the population into the arms of rival parties or of the government. The traditional interplay of qawm and solidarity spaces did not disappear. The precedence of local chiefs had to be respected. Moreover, Massoud kept his hands off economic and social matters (save for the building of schools), the hard core of civil identity. In fact, state-building touched only a very limited sector of society: the politico-military. Elsewhere, civil society was totally autonomous, particularly for logistics—an astonishing phenomenon in such a militarized system. Arms were brought in by lapis lazuli carriers (a local resource), who made the outward trip empty and hence were willing to load weaponry (but did not hesitate to go on strike for higher freight rates).

The Massoud model demonstrated its effectiveness: It conquered all northeast Afghanistan and fought the only real battles in the whole Afghan war, despite the hostility manifested against this system by the Pakistanis, the Hizb-i Islami, and the Pashtun nationalist circles.

The Massoud example represents the only serious break in the Afghan War with both traditional warfare and with jihad as simply an ethical imperative, not a military strategy. Did Massoud's methods do more? Did they set the stage for political modernization and nation-state building in Afghanistan? That remains to be considered in Chapter Six. But, first, an examination of the Afghan mujahidin movement in the larger context of the Muslim world is needed.

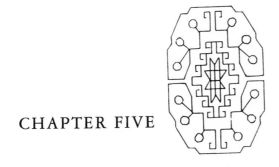

CHAPTER FIVE

AFGHANISTAN
AND THE
WORLD ISLAMIC REVIVAL

ALTHOUGH THE AFGHAN ISLAMIST MOVEMENTS were heavily influenced by the thought and organization of Arab Muslim Brothers, the former's jihad, at least until 1985, had little impact on Arab public opinion. At the time, public opinion was mainly preoccupied with the Israeli-Palestinian conflict or with Iranian radical circles, which dubbed most Afghan resistance parties as "conservative" or even "reactionary." Of course, Iran and most of the Arab countries condemned the Soviet invasion and demanded a Soviet withdrawal. An emergency summit of the Organization of the Islamic Conference was convened in Islamabad on January 1980 to strongly condemn the invasion, but this support came from conservative states (Egypt, Saudi Arabia) and was limited. The mujahidin were not given the Afghanistan seat at the Conference. The Afghan War remained for years almost unnoticed in Muslim world public opinion. The situation changed around 1985. A joint venture between the Saudis, on one side, and the Muslim Brothers and Pakistani Jama'at-i Islami, on the other, had been established, whose objectives were:

1) To promote the more radical Islamist parties among the mujahidin;

2) To check Iranian influence;

3) To prevent Western cultural influences from spreading among refugees and the mujahidin.

The first two objectives had the full support of the Pakistani ISI and of the CIA, which was charged with delivering American military supplies, although both sought to remain in the background behind their chosen proxies.

The Saudi and Islamist joint venture continued until the second Gulf War between the Western coalition and Saddam Husayn, when most Islamists broke with the Saudis. But this

79

joint venture had the effect of pulling Islamism towards a more conservative brand of fundamentalism, which I call "neofundamentalism." The new elite brought forward by the Islamist movement abandoned its revolutionary and political ideology and returned to the sole program of implementing the shari'a.

We shall now look at the different foreign fundamentalist groups who supported the mujahidin, examining their motives and the effect of their actions.

Jama'at-i Islami of Pakistan. Founded by Abu al-Ala Maududi in 1941, in India, the Jama'at is both a political party and a religious association whose aim is to infiltrate elites and to establish an Islamic state.[1] Its electoral performance in Pakistan (about 2.5 percent of the votes) is no measure of its actual influence. Jama'at has been very influential in the circles around the late General Zia al-Haqq. The Jama'at is not a clerical party; indeed, it usually opposes the traditional ulama, who have generally joined two different parties named Jami'at al-Ulama. Nevertheless, General Zia granted the status of "madrasa" to Jama'at University in Mansura (Lahore), in order to upgrade Jama'at's Islamic credentials.

The Jama'at was influential among Afghan intellectual circles in the 1960s, when the Pakistani Pashtun, Qazi Hussayn Ahmad (now the leader—amir—of the Jama'at), had tried to unify the Afghan Islamist movement. This influence did not go beyond the Faculty of Theology and the Kabul campuses. It mainly reached the intelligentsia, as is usual in Islamist movements. It is noteworthy that an ethnic connection already went along with the ideological bond.

The Jama'at choice from among the mujahidin has always been the Hizb-i Islami of Gulbuddin Hekmatyar. Since the 1960s, the ideological differences between Hizb-i Islami and the Afghan Jam'iyyat have been of little consequence. The preference of the Jama'at for the Hizb-i Islami may have been influenced by ethnic

---

1. See K. Bahadur, *The Jama'at-i Islami of Pakistan*.

ties and strategic considerations, shared by the Pakistani military services, which were also staffed by sympathizers of the Jama'at.

The Ahl-i Hadith. Ahl-i Hadith ("The People of the Hadith") is an offshoot of the Indian subcontinent reformist movement founded by Shah Waliullah in the eighteenth century that took a militant stance under the leadership of Sayyid Ahmad Barelvi (d. 1831) and was, wrongly, dubbed "Wahhabi" by the British.[2] The Ahl-i Hadith movement is a religious school that advocates a return to the Qur'ān and Sunna, refuses to acknowledge the four legal schools of Sunni Islam (*mazhab*), and strongly condemns Sufism and Shi'ism. The son of Shah Waliullah and religious disciple of Sayyid Barelvi, Abdul Aziz Dahlavi (d. 1924), authored an anti-Shi'i pamphlet, *Tohfe Asna Ashari'a* (in Persian), which was republished in Turkey in 1988 and widely distributed in Peshawar. The Ahl-i Hadith advocates the right of ijtihad, or interpretation. It parted company with the Hanafi school on specific and subtle theological issues, such as the way to pray. For Afghan orthodox Hanafis, this innovation in praying amounts to heresy. Although strongly reformist and fundamentalist, Ahl-i Hadith has never been political-minded. For example, it did not fight British domination in India.

In Pakistan today, the Ahl-i Hadith is both a religious movement and a political party. Contrary to the Jama'at, it did not directly support General Zia and opposed the Shariat Bill (on the ground that it is not up to the state to legislate on the shari'a). Its leader, Ehsan Illahi Zaher, was assassinated in Lahore in 1987.

The Ahl-i Hadith networks were heavily supported by the Saudi Wahhabis during the 1980s; hence, it is no longer irrelevant to call it "Wahhabi." The Ahl-i Hadith, in any case, has more in common with Wahhabism than with the Muslim Brothers or Maududi's ideology.

2. M. Hedayetullah, *A Study of the Religious Reform Movement of Sayyid Ahmad.* See also Barbara Metcalf, *Islamic Revival in British India.*

The Ahl-i Hadith has been very active in the Northwest Frontier Province since the nineteenth century. It established madrasas in Attok, Akora, and in the Kunar Valley (in the village of Panjpir: hence one of its Afghan names, "panjpiri"). Its preaching spread into Afghanistan in the 1950s among local mullahs, mainly in border areas. Because of the lack of suitable madrasas, it was customary for Afghan mullahs to go to India for training. After the Partition, in 1947, many Afghan religious students joined madrasas established in the nearby Northwest Frontier Province. They were mainly Pashtu-speakers, but also Nuristanis and Badakhshis. Some of them converted to the Ahl-i Hadith ideology. When back in Afghanistan, they fought against Sufism and Hanafism, for example, by destroying local *zyarat* (tombs of holy men). They used to be dubbed "Wahhabi" by the Hanafis, but called themselves "Salafi." Relations between them and the traditional Hanafi mullahs were tense and led to local armed feuds.

The Soviet invasion gave political visibility to the small Ahl-i Hadith pockets in Afghanistan because they enjoyed direct financial support from their Pakistani sponsors, soon supplemented by Saudi Wahhabi direct financing. These "Wahhabi" amirates are: Barg-i Matal in Northern Nuristan; the Pech Valley in Kunar; and the Argo district in Badakhshan. Interestingly enough, the "amirates" usually coincide with local tribal or ethnic divisions. Mawlawi Afzal of Barg-i Matal, educated first at Deoband (India), then at Akora (Pakistan), taught in an Ahl-i Hadith madrasa in Karachi, then opened his own in Badmuk, his native village. At the outbreak of the insurrection of 1978, he ousted the Hizb-i Islami local leader (Obeydullah) and converted his own tribe, the Kâtis, to Wahhabism. The rival southern tribe, the Kâm, under Mawlawi Rustam, remained with Hizb-i Islami. Mawlawi Afzal founded his "Islamic State of Afghanistan," known locally as the "Dawlat." In 1987, a young Libyan named "Sulayman," coming from Saudi Arabia, was the Arab representative in Barg-i Matal, the main city of the "Dawlat."

In Badakhshan, Mawlawi Hamidullah, educated in Panjpir and Karachi, founded a madrasa in the sixties. One of his students, Mawlawi Shariqi, joined the Jam'iyyat-i Islami at the outbreak of the war. He later split with the party and established his own "Wahhabi" amirate around Argo, whose influence at its peak went from Jurm to Shahr-i Bozorg. It included many Tajiks but also Uzbek "muhajir" (who emigrated from the Soviet Union in the 1930s). Shariqi was killed in Peshawar in 1984. His group, led by Mawlawi Jamal Nasser, Danushi, Sayyid Ali, and Kheyratmand, joined the Hizb-i Islami and constantly fought against the Jam'iyyat. Occasionally, it even sided with the government. In the summer of 1991 they were defeated and expelled by Massoud.

In Kunar, Mawlawi Jamilurrahman, educated in Peshawar in the Salasin Madrasa, also founded a "Wahhabi" republic in the Pech Valley, after seceding from the Hizb-i Islami. He founded the "Hizb al-da'wat" and brought with him most of the Pashtun Safi subtribe of the Pech Valley, while the Hizb-i Islami retained the loyalty of most of the Shinwari and Meshwani Pashtun tribes. In 1991, heavy fighting pitted the two groups against each other for control of the liberated province of Kunar. Mawlawi Jamilurrahman was assassinated, but his followers, with Saudi support, succeeded in gaining control of the provincial capital, Asadabad.

It is noteworthy that in all the foregoing cases religious splits coincided with ethnic and tribal rifts.

Saudi Arabia. The Saudi government supported the mujahid movement from the beginning of the war; apparently, it maintained relations with all parties. Gaylani, a moderate and rather secular leader, has a Saudi passport; and all the leaders used to be welcome in Riyadh. In fact, however, it soon became obvious that the Saudis were supporting the more radical Islamists. This policy was initiated by different centers of Saudi influence, each using its own network: the Wahhabi clergy, the government, the personal intervention of different princes and notables. The religious Wahhabi circles, close to Shaykh ibn Baz, head of the Saudi Council of Ulama, were motivated by their anti-Shi'i and anti-Sufi bias. They supported leaders or local commanders on the sole basis of their theological positions. They heavily subsidized A. Sayyaf but also supported local commanders sponsored by the Ahl-i Hadith. The channels for choosing the "right commanders" were mainly Saudi-trained Afghan mullahs, who tended to adopt part, if not all, of the Wahhabi philosophy. Thus, the nickname "Wahhabi" given by local Afghan and Pakistani populations to any scripturalist reformist movement tended to become more and more accurate.

Religious legitimacy has always been crucial for the Saudi dynasty, which has for long endeavored to gain the support of moderate Islamists, specifically, of the main branch of the Muslim Brothers, in order to fight against progressive and nationalist revolutionary trends, such as Ba'thism and Nasserism. The World Islamic League (Rabita), founded in 1962, with headquarters in Mecca, was created to develop a modern and reformist fundamentalism, acceptable to non-Wahhabi fundamentalist circles, politically conservative but culturally anti-Western. The Rabita is made up of organizations, not states; the General Secretary is a Saudi (since 1983, Doctor Abdullah Omar Nassif). With a huge budget, the Rabita trains mullahs and subsidizes mosques, libraries, and organizations. The Rabita has been the bridge between the Muslim Brothers and Wahhabis. The emergence since the 1960s of a radical trend among Islamists, under the influence of Sayyid Qutb, put the Saudi monarchy in an awkward situation. It was challenged in the name of Islam. The Iranian Islamic Revolution of 1979 was violently opposed to the House of Saud and made matters worse. The Saudi response has not been to shy away from fundamentalism but, on the contrary, to increase support for radical Sunni Islamists in order to accentuate the gap between Sunnism and Shi'ism and thus prevent the spread of the Iranian Revolution outside of Shi'i areas.

In addition to the Wahhabi clergy and the Saudi government, a third center active in shaping Saudi policy towards Pakistan has been the Saudi external secret service headed by Prince Turki ibn Faysal, who chose to support Gulbuddin Hekmatyar, more for strategic than ideological reasons, as we shall see.

The Saudi breakthrough among the mujahidin had mixed and contradictory results. Most of the leaders and local commanders took the money but, except for the "Wahhabi" amirates already mentioned, did not adhere to the Wahhabi doctrine and remained more under the political influence of the Muslim Brothers than of the Saudis. Wahhabism as a doctrine has never been very popular among traditional Sunni Muslims. Moreover, radical Islamists have always been critical of Saudi Arabia ("There is no king in Islam," as opponents of the monarchy used to say).

The Arab Muslim Brothers. The influence of the Muslim Brothers goes back to the 1960s, when future professors of the Faculty of Theology were studying at al-Azhar University in Cairo (Gholam Niazi and Burhanuddin Rabbani). Returning to Afghanistan, they founded the Jam'iyyat-i Islami of Afghanistan, which has been followed by the movement of the Young Muslims (Jawanan-i Mosalman).[3] Translations of Sayyid Qutb's work were widely distributed on Afghan campuses.

In the early years following the Soviet invasion of Afghanistan, however, support from Arab Islamic circles for the mujahidin was low. Their main support came from governments that were at odds with radical Islamists: Egypt's Anwar al-Sadat, for example, shipped weapons to them. The association of the mujahidin with regimes unfriendly to the Arabs and with the West was an obstacle to close relations. Another factor is a persistent ethnocentrism in the Arab world. The Muslim Brothers, for example, is an Arab organization, which, despite its claim to address the whole Islamic umma, recruits almost exclusively among Arabs.

After 1984, however, support for the mujahidin began to come from Arab sources. This took the form of a joint venture between Wahhabi circles from Riyadh and the Muslim Brothers: Riyadh provided the money; the Brothers, the staff and the brains.

The Brothers' cadres active in Afghanistan were predominantly Palestinians with Jordanian passports. The Jordanian branch of the society, headed by Muhammad Abdurrahman Khalifa, seems to have played a larger role in the support for the Afghan jihad than did the Egyptian center. They established an office in Peshawar as early as 1982, headed by Abdullah Ezzam, himself a Palestinian with a Jordanian passport who married an Afghan woman. An efficient and dedicated organizer, Ezzam traveled extensively in Afghanistan and tried tirelessly to unite

3. See Roy, *Islam and Resistance*, Chap. 4.

Hizb-i Islami and the Jam'iyyat-i Islami, while always favoring the former under the leadership of Hekmatyar. After a trip to meet Massoud in the summer of 1989, he endeavored to strike a balanced attitude between the two parties, but he was assassinated in November 1989 in a very sophisticated terrorist action whose authors were never discovered.

To publicize the Afghan jihad in Arab circles, Ezzam published *Al-Jihâd*, a journal in Arabic. He endeavored to coordinate Islamic help for the mujahidin. An increasing number of Muslim humanitarian organizations were established in Peshawar, from the Saudi Red Crescent to Sudanese relief agencies, whose aim was also to marginalize Western nongovernment organizations accused of being a cover for Christian missionary activity. Abdullah Ezzam also helped to establish a kind of "Islamic Legion." The idea was not only to support the Afghan jihad but also to establish in Afghanistan a new brand of fundamentalism, opposing both cultural traditions (tribalism) and religious ones (Hanafism, Sufism). As a Saudi journalist put it: "The Muslim scholars of the world have a great role to play in enlightening the ignorant Afghans. Un-Islamic customs and traditions have found their way into their lives."[4]

Arab advisers were influential in Peshawar among all the Islamist parties. They usually supported a faction inside each party (for example, the Nurullah Emmat group within the Jam'iyyat-i Islami), thus enlarging the already existing discrepancy between the more pragmatist field commanders and the Peshawar bureaucracy, which recruited among the exiled intelligentsia and turned more and more conservative and fundamentalist.

The Joint Venture. From 1984 to 1990, the joint venture of the Saudis, the Muslim Brothers, and the Pakistani military secret services (ISI) channeled the bulk of military aid to Gulbuddin Hekmatyar and sought to advance him politically. Wahhabi cir-

---

4. *Arab News*, September 14, 1985, "Afghan Mujahedeen Fight to Defend their Faith, Country," by Abdullah al-Rifae, p. 9. This article also contains direct attacks against Western volunteer relief agencies, dubbed "Christian missionaries."

cles preferred at the beginning to support Sayyaf and local commanders through Ahl-i Hadith. Sayyaf has been said to be himself a Wahhabi, probably wrongly despite the fact that he changed his name Abdurrasul ("slave of the Prophet") to Abdul Rabb Rassul ("slave of the Lord of the Prophet"), which is a typical Wahhabi denial of any divinity in the Prophet; but he is also said to be the only non-Arab member of the Supreme Council of the Muslim Brotherhood. In any case, Sayyaf's attitude during the Gulf War showed him to be closer to the Muslim Brothers than to the Saudis.

Another discrepancy is the support, although rather small, given to Massoud by some moderate Muslim Brothers, despite the fact that the Pakistanis have constantly opposed his rise. Even so, there was, in general, a relatively coherent ISI/Saudi and Muslim Brothers joint venture from 1982 to 1990.

What was behind this joint venture? First, an ideological commitment. The Pakistani Jama'at-i Islami shares the same ideology as the Muslim Brothers, and the ISI has always been close to the Jama'at. The Saudis were quite distant from the political interpretation of Islam common to al-Banna and Maududi but were endeavoring, with the foundation of the Rabita, to find common ground with the moderate Brothers. The rapprochement between the Wahhabis and the Islamists was accelerated by the outbreak of the Iran-Iraq War and the Soviet invasion of Afghanistan. Saudi strategy throughout the 1980s was to strengthen a radical Sunni fundamentalist camp in order to counterbalance the impact of the Iranian Revolution among the Muslim masses. The Saudis, lacking personnel, let the Muslim Brothers be active in the field, and the latter chose their partners among those most closely related to them ideologically.

Still, this is not enough to explain why Sayyaf and Hekmatyar have been the main beneficiaries of the aid, not Rabbani, whose Islamist credentials are as strong, if not stronger. The reason is more strategic than ideological. The ISI and Saudi Prince Turki chose to support the Pashtuns and to shun the Tajiks, thought to be potentially prone, as Persian-speakers, to accept Iranian influence.

The Pakistani choice of Hekmatyar had a strategic background. They wanted:

• To pull the rug from under Iran's feet, by supporting a Pashtun Sunni radical Islamism against both the Shi'a and the Tajiks.

• To control the Pashtun tribal belt inside Afghanistan, in order to obtain strategic depth against the Indian threat.

• To avoid the rise of any strong central Afghan state that could challenge Islamabad's control of the tribal belt and establish a strategic axis with India, as Prince Daoud did in the 1950s.

• To fill the vacuum left by the Soviet withdrawal, even from Central Asia, in order to create a Sunni conservative and fundamentalist entity among Iran, India, and Russia, thus recreating the ghost of the Moghul Empire.

To achieve this complex set of goals, Islamabad played on the ethnic segmentation in Afghanistan, favoring the Ghilzay Pashtun against both the Durrani Pashtun (tribal base of the former monarchy) and the Persian-speakers, whether Sunni or Shi'a. A final element must be mentioned: Hekmatyar has been close to the ISI ever since his 1974 exile in Pakistan, and this situation has allowed the ISI to think that any government established around him will be closer to Pakistan.

Religious, strategic, political, and ideological motivations were interwoven to such an extent that it is sometimes difficult to understand the choices made by foreign fundamentalists. The different sponsors of the mujahidin joined their efforts in a more or less coherent policy but used multiple channels of supply and communications with the mujahidin: individuals, factions inside the parties, parties, and local commanders. In fact, under the pretext of choosing "good Muslims," the sponsors often established their own direct channels of support in the form of a patron-client relationship. This accentuated the already existing divisions among the mujahidin.

The Islamic Legion. Thousands of volunteers from all over the Muslim world came to wage their personal jihad in Afghanistan. Most of them were Arabs, but Turks and Kurds also came. Although they came through Muslim Brothers channels, supervised in Peshawar by Abdullah Ezzam, there has been no military "Islamic headquarters" in Pakistan. The Pakistan Army succeeded in maintaining responsibility for "advising" the mujahidin. Inside Afghanistan, Arab volunteers played a more or less political role because of their prestige, dedication to armed action, and amount of money they carried with them. Arab advisers have been influential with such commanders as Haqqani in Paktya and Alam Khan in Balkh; but they failed to keep out Western aid-workers and journalists. Most local mujahidin commanders were able to control the activities of Arab volunteers, not hesitating to expel the most fanatic (as Ismail Khan did in the West), all the more so because their fanaticism and scorning of Afghan traditions, dubbed "un-Islamic," antagonized the population. Some of these volunteers have massacred prisoners of war, and, according to some sources, abducted women of progovernment militiamen, making it more difficult for regime soldiers to defect.

The volunteers trained in Afghan mujahidin camps were not devoted solely to the Afghan jihad. From 1987 on, radical foreign Islamist groups sent trainees to Afghanistan in order to return later and wage jihad in their own countries. This is true for mujahidin of the Hizbullah in Kashmir, of the Moros Liberation Front in the Philippines, of Turks and Palestinians, and also of Algerians. In December 1991, for example, an armed group of such radicals was annihilated by the Algerian Army near El Souk. This splinter group from FIS (Islamic Salvation Front) was led by one Tayyib "Al-Afghani," whose sobriquet indicated his Afghan combat experience. Afghanistan veterans are nowadays the hard core of the radical Islamist movements all over the Middle East.

Since 1990, the main training site has been the Jaji camp in Paktya Province, under the auspices of the Hizb-i Islami of Hekmatyar.

Thus the Saudi/Muslim Brothers/ISI joint venture, established under American auspices with the aim of distributing American military supplies, has in fact strengthened and trained radical and anti-Western Islamists throughout the Muslim world.[5]

The Aftermath of the Gulf War. The bulk of the Muslim Brothers condemned a Saudi request for Western troops to protect

5. On United States policy, see O. Roy, "The Lessons of the Soviet-Afghan War."

Holy Places within their country, with the exception, of course, of the Kuwaitis, while the Wahhabi clergy gave a *fatwa* approving the call for foreign troops. The ensuing split extended to Afghanistan: Sayyaf and Hekmatyar openly chose Saddam Husayn against the Saudi monarchy. Even the head of the Pakistan Army, General Alsan Beg, made a statement against the Saudi request for Western support. This attitude from movements that got most of their funds from Riyadh came as a shock to the Saudis. The only support they got from Afghan mujahidin came from people they had shunned: B. Rabbini, leader of the JIA, and S. Mojaddidi, a moderate leader.

The Gulf War revealed the Saudi failure to attract Islamism under their own conservative banner. The alliance betweeen Hekmatyar and the Muslim Brothers or other extremist Islamist groups has been strengthened by the Gulf War.

The Saudis then began a reassessment of their policy towards Islamist groups and cut supplies to most of them, beginning with the Algerian FIS. But the Saudi policy reassessment led to tensions between a part of the Wahhabi clergy (led by Shaykh ibn Baz, chairman of the Saudi Council of Ulama) and the monarchy. Thus, the Saudis chose . . . not to choose. After the fall of Kabul, in May 1992, and the subsequent refusal of Hekmatyar to join the newly established mujahidin coalition government, the Saudis tried hard to bring Hekmatyar back into the coalition. Semiofficial and private Wahhabi networks interfered in Afghanistan to accentuate the "re-Islamization" of the country and supported Hekmatyar and Sayyaf. Afghanistan highlights the main Saudi contradiction: Strategically allied with the West, the Saudis support religious and cultural networks fighting against Western presence and influence.

The Pakistanis, and more particularly the civilian government of Prime Minister Nawaz Sharif, became aware of the danger of being bound to extremist groups. General Beg's retirement led to less support for Hekmatyar. Yet, there has been no drastic change in Pakistani policy, which can be more accurately called a "bilevel" policy. The military wanted to ensure an indirect control of the tribal belt through local commanders, while civilians wished to sign an overall agreement with Moscow in order to put an end to the war and have a free hand for an overall

Central Asian policy. In any case, ties between local commanders and Hekmatyar on one hand and the Pakistani military officers and local officials on the other are so strong that it is almost impossible to sever them. Drug trafficking is not the least important aspect of this collaboration.

A New Brand of Fundamentalism

The Afghan mujahidin movement embodied the shift, widespread in the Muslim world, from a political and revolutionary Islam to a conservative brand of fundamentalism, although the sociological basis of this "neofundamentalism" is quite different from that of the older brand, which explains the use we make of the term. The new militants are from the intelligentsia, not from the clerical rank, even though they tend to compete for control of the mosques. It is not rare to see secular-educated students achieving an accelerated training as "mullahs" either in an autodidactic way or through the "missionary" institutes established by the Wahhabis, the Ahl-i Hadith, the Pakistani Jama'at, or the Jama'at al-Tabligh, a nonpolitical Indo-Pakistani association founded in the 1920s. These self-proclaimed mullahs have retained from their Islamist background the demand for an Islamic state, political activism, millenarianism (instead of revolution), claiming that Islam and only Islam will solve all problems. But their sole program today is the same as that of the mullahs—implementation of the shari'a. They want to reshape and unite the Sunni Muslim umma within the framework of a purified Islam, while getting rid of national, traditional, and cultural accretions. Their quest for an ethical model (that is, the imitation of the Prophet without reference to history, literature, local culture, and traditions; in a word, without reference to the age-old Muslim culture) has given birth to a new, universal model of the "Islamic militant" from Algeria to Pakistan with the same looks, gestures, references—and vacuity of thought.

This "re-Islamization" found a favorable ground in Afghanistan among a secular-educated youth that chose Islam as an ideology and was fighting against the old establishment, either composed of the tribal aristocracy associated with local "khans" or of the ulama, whose earlier strength as institutionalized in the traditional educational system was almost completely destroyed by the war. The only working educational system for the Afghans is now the new schools established among refugees in Pakistan. Although these schools are often financed by the United Nations or Western aid agencies, they are controlled by this new intelligentsia, influenced by the Wahhabi and Muslim Brothers ideology.

There has been a cultural crisis of identity throughout the war, which has given way to this neofundamentalism. Sufism was already in decay among urban circles before the war (but paradoxically extending to some remote regions like the Aimaq area) and has been severely undermined by revolution and war (executions of pir, lack of adequate training for youth). The teaching of traditional Persian literature and Muslim philosophy almost came to a halt due to the poor level of the few remaining high schools and colleges. The patterns of traditional society—tribalism, power of local notables, and even ethnic references—were also shaken and altered by the war. The ideologization of Islam by young intellectuals has been a response to this crisis and was seen as a way of modernization.

Political Islam, however, has been unable to supersede the traditional segmentation of society and provide a workable alternative. There is no way, in political Islam, to conceive segmentation otherwise than as personal failure, lack of faith, obscurantism, or as a foreign plot. There is no Islamic sociology. It is easier for political Islam to adopt mathematics and physics than anthropology and ethnology. Traditional politics, which could not be conceptualized in an Islamic political framework, has returned in force.

Iran Between Exclusive Support for the Shi'is and Pragmatism

The Shi'a and Politics in Afghanistan. The Shi'a probably constitute about 12 percent of the Afghan population, although they claim to account for 30 percent.[6] They are mainly Hazara, a Persian-speaking ethnic group living in the central part of Afghanistan. The Hazara came under the control of the Kabul central government in 1892. Most are usually poor peasants, dominated by *arbab* or *mir* (i.e., landowners) and sayyid (descendants of the Prophet Muhammad), who are far more venerated in Hazarajat than elsewhere in Afghanistan. In Kabul, Hazara tend to be porters, cooks, and cleaners, but a minority of them has succeeded in becoming rich traders. Hazara are generally despised by Sunni Afghans. They in turn resent what appears to them as Pashtun colonialism in their lands, through the combined intrusion of the central administration and nomads, who bought or seized lands for pasture. The Hazara have been barred from high positions both in the army and the government on account of their ethnicity. During the 1970s, tens of thousands of Hazara went to Iran as laborers.

In the cities, other Shi'a groups are to be found. The Kizilbash in Kabul, as in Kandahar, are probably descendants of Iranian soldiers and civil officers established in the mid-seventeenth century. Both assimilated in terms of language, but kept a strong Shi'a identity. In Herat, the Shi'a population seems to be indigenous, Herat having been a part of the Safavid Empire at one time. Urban Shi'a are well educated and assimilated.

Afghan Shi'a used to identify with Iran, in order to counterbalance the hostility of the Sunni environment. Pictures of the Shah were to be found in the 1960s, where Khumayni's pictures are to be seen now. As early as the 1950s, a revivalist movement took place within their community. A new Shi'a clergy, well-educated and activist, seems to have regained some influence in the community at that time. (King Zahir, however, did try to strengthen traditional Hazara leaders mainly through elections to the National Assembly in the 1960s.) This new clergy acquired legitimacy through its direct link with the Iranian ayatollahs established in Najaf. Traditional identification with Iran and

6. On the Afghan Shi'a and their politicization, see David B. Edwards, "Shi'a Political Dissent in Afghanistan."

religious legitimacy were thus merged. It is not clear when young Afghan clerics found their way to Najaf and Kerbala, but such a move began in the 1950s and persisted until the Iran-Iraq War. Young clerics went to Najaf and Kerbala, whereas some lay Hazara emigrants went to Iran and Iraq in search of employment, finding sometimes the opportunity to study there as well. A milieu of émigrés, both secular and clerical, was thus created, which became highly politicized and influenced by contemporary political debates. Most of the present cadres of the Shi'a movement in Afghanistan are offsprings of this generation, politicized between 1960 and 1980.

The travels of Afghan Shi'a in Iran and Iraq has led to their recent Iranization. As noted by Edwards and Kopecki, typical Iranian Shi'a rituals (e.g., use of tape-recorded sermons on Husayn's battle against oppressors during the holy month of *muharram*) seem to have been introduced in Afghanistan from the 1950s on.[7] A recent "Iranization" of the Afghan Shi'a community is obvious in other aspects as well, such as in the use of certain names and patronyms ("agha," or mister, and patronyms ending in "i," like Beheshti, Tavasolli, instead of Mirza Husseyn, etc.), which were common a generation ago. The spread of revivalist ideas dates back to 1950, when Sayyad Ismail Balkhi, a cleric recently returned from Qum, engaged in politicoreligious itinerant preaching and was arrested. Other Shi'a clerics became active in the sixties, such as Wa'ez in Kabul or Shaykh Muhseni in Kandahar. All these figures shared an approach that had two important characteristics:

1) Their politicoreligious activities preceded the Iranian Revolution: The radicalization of the Afghan Shi'a community is not a consequence of the Iranian Revolution but is part of a broader Shi'a movement whose center was in Najaf and Kerbala rather than in Qum;[8]

---

7. Lucas-Michael Kopecky, "The Imami Sayyad of the Hazarajat," pp. 91 and 95. See also Edwards, p. 214.

8. See O. Roy, "Les Frontières de l'Iran."

2) They were mainly disciples of Ayatollah Hakim, until his death in 1970, then of ayatollahs Khuy or Shariat-Madari, and only to a lesser extent of Ayatollah Khumayni. The two highest-ranking living Shi'a clerics in Afghanistan, Shaykh Muhseni (head of the Harakat-i Islami, or "Islamic Movement") and Qorban Ali Mohaqeq (from Turkman Valley), who is now in Iran and not involved in politics, are disciples of Ayatollah Khuy. Only the third cleric in the present hierarchy, the lesser known Taghadossi, is a disciple of Khumayni. Also from Turkman, he now heads the Afghan Pasdaran, or "Guardians."

Another important element is that the Shi'a youth were influenced also by leftist (Maoist) and nationalist movements. Curiously enough, there was no clear-cut distinction between leftist, nationalist, and clerical movements among the Hazara, contrary to the Sunni. The reason is that all these movements, except for those espoused by a few clerics like Muhseni, who is not an ethnic Hazara, expressed first a Hazara identity. This explains why, at the outset of the upheaval against the Communist regime, the Hazara were the only ethnic group to establish a political organization on an "ethnic" base, the Shura-yi Inqilabi-yi Ittifaq-i Islami-yi Afghanistan.

At the time of the Communist coup of 1978, several political parties were established among the Shi'a on both an ideological and ethnic base:

• Sazman-i Nasr, created by Shaykh Mazari and Siddiqi from Nili: a radical, revolutionary organization, which recruited among the Hazara intelligentsia in Iran and is said to have included many former young leftists and Hazara nationalists. Sazman-i Nasr fought against traditional notables and landowners, some of whom have been executed, like Haji Nader in Turkman Valley. The party is headed by a council.

• Harakat-i Islami (not to be confused with the Sunni Harakat-i Inqilab-i Islami), founded in 1979 by Shaykh Asaf Muhseni, a cleric from Kandahar and disciple of Ayatollah Khuy. It recruits among urban Shi'a, mainly Kizilbash. Its relations with Iran have never been good. In 1979, Muhseni, then established in Iran, was put under house arrest, following the seizure of American documents advocating support for him. In January

1988, Muhseni left for Peshawar, refusing to join the newly established Hizb-i Wahdat.

• Shura-yi Inqilabi-yi Ittifaq-i Islami-yi Afghanistan, or "Islamic United Council of Afghanistan," was created by traditional clerics (like Sayyid Ali Beheshti), *mir* (landowners, also called *arbab*), and intellectuals, in the summer of 1979, when the Hazarajat was almost entirely freed from any government presence (except Bamyan, which was evacuated by the Communists in the summer of 1988). Although the Shura never acknowledged its purely Hazara or Shi'a identity, it was more nationalist-minded than clerical.

These three groups were rivals. Shura and Nasr waged a bloody civil war from 1982 to 1984.

• Hizbullah: a group created in 1979 among the Shi'a of the city of Herat and headed by Qari Yekdast.

Iran's Policy Towards Afghanistan. Iran's policy was twofold: to unite and control the Shi'a under a more or less direct Iranian supervision, then to use the Shi'a card to bargain with the other protagonists, mainly Moscow and Islamabad, in order to see its patronage recognized and to avoid the coming to power of a Saudi-supported Sunni regime in Kabul.[9] Tehran never played the ethnic card (Persian-speakers against Pashtuns) but only the religious card. Rivalries among the Iranian Pasdaran, the office of Ayatollah Montazeri in Qum, and the Ministry of Foreign Affairs led to some confusion among the groups supported by Tehran. A civil war opposed Shura and Nasr, from 1982 to 1984, and Nasr against Sepah from 1985 to 1987.

The Iranian Pasdaran Headquarters decided to create a sister organization in Afghanistan, through a split in the Shura and in Nasr. Sepah-i Pasdaran was founded under direct Iranian supervision around 1982. Apparently, it was an endeavor by the Iranian Pasdaran to bypass the political divisions among Afghan Shi'a by bringing together all pro-Iranian elements in a single movement.

9. For an excellent presentation of Iranian policy toward Afghanistan, see Zalmay Khalilzad, "Iranian Revolution and Afghan Resistance."

PLATES

1. An official welcome for Ismail Khan (in white), with a military parade marking the second anniversary of the independence of Turkmenistan (Ashghabad, Turkmenistan, 27 October 1993). Most of the Russian officers who are parading fought in Afghanistan: Geopolitics have won over ideology.

2. Massoud in discussion with a traditional Qazi, Panjshir Valley (1982).

3. Ismail Khan (left) with a traditional notable (turban) and a civil servant (Astrakhan cap), in the liberated suburbs of Herat (1982).

4. A tea-house in the liberated areas of Paktya (1982), where the owner displays posters of almost all mujahidin political parties in order to please all patrons.

5. A "political predicant," with horse and loudspeaker, making *da'wa* in the liberated areas north of Kabul (1981).

6. Students of a religious school (madrasa) belonging to the "Chestiyya" brotherhood in liberated areas near Chest-i Sharif, Herat Province, 1982.

7. A traditional *"alim"*: Mawlawi Mirajauiddin, from Astana (Panjshir), who helped Massoud establish his power in the Panjshir Valley; he studied in an Indian madrasa in the forties and had accumulated hundreds of books and manuscripts, which were later destroyed during a Soviet offensive.

1

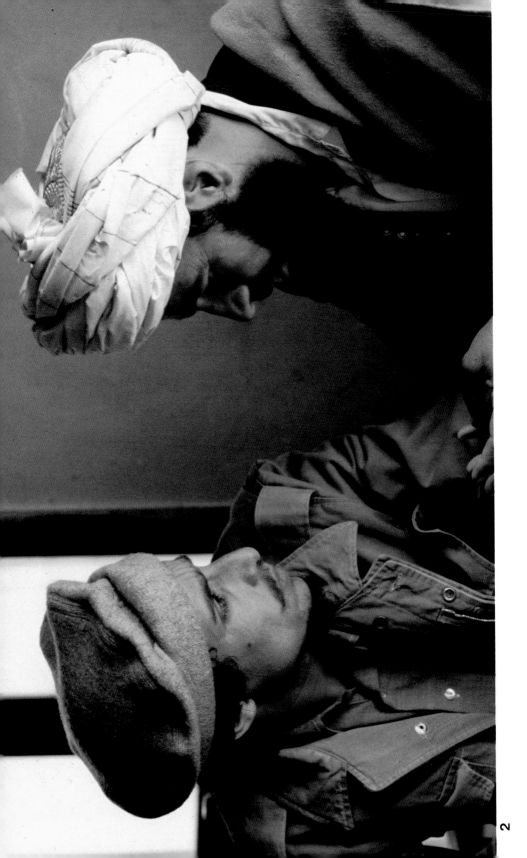

4

As is usual in Afghanistan, the structure created to unite the other parties became one more party among the others. Sepah came into existence as a splinter group from the Shura, headed by two clerics, Akbari from Behsud and Siddiqi from Nili. Sepah has the same ideology as Nasr, but has more clerical cadres.

The second endeavor to unite the Shi'a was done under the auspices of the clerical milieux of Qum. An "Eight-Party Alliance" was established in Qum, grouping all the pro-Iranian Shi'a parties and excluding the Shura.

The last and most successful achievement was in the summer of 1989, when most of the Shi'a parties, including the Shura, united in a new Hizb-i Wahdat, encouraged to do so by the Iranian Ministry of Foreign Affairs. The difference is that this party has been founded without any ideological referent. The common ground is in fact "nationalist": The followers are all Hazara. The Hazara of Harakat-i Islami joined it, whereas the non-Hazara (and Muhseni himself) refused to do so. Internecine feuds occurred between Hizb-i Wahdat and the Harakat, reduced to the Kizilbash constituency. Siddiqi of Nili, a figurehead of Hizb-i Wahdat, was assassinated in November 1990. The head of Hizb-i Wahdat is Shaykh Mazari, a Hazara from northern Afghanistan.

The disappearance of ideological references in the Afghan Shi'a movement has been made possible by the supremacy of the pragmatists in Tehran against the radicals (headed by Mohtashemi), who nevertheless never made Afghanistan a priority in their foreign activities.

Iran and the Afghan Sunni. There has been some Iranian influence among the Afghan Sunni, but in cultural, not political, terms. Revolutionary rhetoric has pervaded all mujahidin discourse: Even conservative mullahs call the rising against the Communists a "revolution." Pictorial symbols were borrowed from Iran (e.g., tulips for *shahid*, "martyrs"); Iranian customs and expressions, due to long sojourns in Iran (and also to listening to the popular BBC Persian Service), became more common. But as a general rule, identifying Iran with Shi'ism has prevented the Iranian political model from spreading among Sunnis.

Iranian policy toward Sunni mujahidin has been ambiguous. Without formally condemning the Peshawar alliance, Iran, until 1988, made a distinction between "Islamic" parties (that is, "Islamists") and "reactionary" parties (so-called moderates), condemning any attempt to reach an agreement with the Soviets or to bring back former King Zahir. The Iranian media referred to mujahidin as "Afghan revolutionary Muslims," thus avoiding allusions to particular political and ethnic groups. Iran asked the Sunnis to adopt a "neither East nor West" policy and condemned their reliance on Western arms shipments, stressing the priority of revolution over short-term military gains. In fact, however, Iran has never provided direct support even to Sunni "Islamic" mujahidin (Massoud's Jam'iyyat or the two Hizb parties, that of Hekmatyar and the Kahlis splinter group). The official distinction between "Islamic" and "reactionary" parties meant only that the former were allowed to have offices in Tehran.

Instead of giving direct support to Islamist parties, Iran tried to attract Sunni splinter groups. Some local Sunni fighting groups along the Iran-Afghanistan border were organized as Hizbullah groups (it is not clear whether they were part of the Hizbullah that we listed before as a Shi'a party). These Sunni Hizbullah groups (but not the Shi'a) were disbanded by Ismail Khan, of the Jam'iyyat, in the summer of 1986. Iran also welcomed Sunni splinter group leaders, like Nasrullah Mansur (from Harakat-i Inqilab), who was given a warm welcome in December 1987; Mawlawi Mo'azen (from Mojaddidi's National Salvation Front); and Qâzi Amin Wâqêd (a dissident of Hekmatyar's Hizb-i Islami). A local figure from western Afghanistan, the Pir of Obey —who created an organization called Jami'at al-Ulama in 1980 (which was in fact infiltrated by Maoists) and left for Iran after clashes with Jam'iyyat-i Islami—played the token role of Sunni for interviews on Tehran Radio, supporting Iran's position against Saudi Arabia at the end of August 1987. A Jam'iyyat-i Islami splinter group in Herat, headed by Safiullah Afzali, assassinated in July 1987, got more Iranian support than the dominant Jam'iyyat leader, Ismail Khan, although in fact the Afzali group was sponsored by Wahhabi organizations.

It does not seem that Iran really tried to implement a radical

Islamic revolution among Afghan Sunni. Perhaps the Iranians thought that the Sunnis of Afghanistan were politically too backward or that the Afghan Shi'a would be able to "revolutionize" their Sunni brothers without direct Iranian intervention. The most reasonable interpretation is strategic: Iran wanted to keep a foothold and leverage in Afghanistan through the Shi'a, but was not eager to confront the Soviets or to see a premature victory of the mujahidin, which could bring the United States back into the area.

Iran has always been unwilling to encourage the emergence of a strong Sunni resistance and has kept some distance even from the more radical Sunni parties. Members of the Hizb-i Islami left Iran in 1984, disappointed by the lack of support. Today, the Jam'iyyat is the only Sunni party to have an overall representation in Iran. Relations between Iran and the more radical Islamist party, the Hizb, soured considerably in 1991, when an Iranian newspaper called for the assassination of Hekmatyar. The interesting point is that Hekmatyar is linked with the radical Muslim Brothers (like the Sudanese leader Hasan Turabi), whom Tehran courted to build a "refusal front" against the peace process in the Middle East. There seems to be no direct link between an overall Iranian strategy and its Afghan policy, and Tehran has never pursued an ethnic policy in Afghanistan.

Afghan politics, however, remains dominated by the ethnic question. The mainly Persian-speaking Jam'iyyat is one of the few Sunni parties (with Gaylani and Mojaddidi) to have friendly relations with Shi'a and to acknowledge the right of the Shi'a to have their own religious courts. In the field, there is cooperation between Jam'iyyat commanders and the Hizb-i Wahdat. Generally, Afghan Pashtuns are more opposed to the Shi'a, for historical and cultural reasons, than are the Tajik. Hekmatyar and Khalis even deny the right to implement a specific Shi'a system of law.[10] In the south of Hazarajat, relations between Hazara and Pashtuns are based on traditional ethnic feuds. The Qarabagh and Ghazni incidents in August 1988, when heavy clashes occurred between Hazara and Pashtun, were entirely ethnically determined.

10. Personal interview with Hekmatyar, March 1987.

Limited Iranian Influence in Afghanistan. First, in contrast to Lebanon and Iraq, Afghanistan has only a small minority of Shi'a, who are generally despised by other ethnic groups. Sunni ulama have traditionally been rather anti-Shi'a for theological reasons, considering Shi'a as virtual heretics. Influence from Muslim Brothers and Wahhabi milieux, which increased among Afghan mujahidin in the course of the war, did nothing to ease relations between Sunni and Shi'a. The fact that the Shi'a did little fighting against the Soviets and often plundered Sunni convoys made matters worse. Tension between Shi'a and Sunni were in a sense exacerbated by the war.

Second, the main consideration of Iranian policy has been the Middle East and its war with Iraq. In this respect, Iran needed leverage over the Soviets, but was careful to avoid direct or even indirect confrontation. The solution was to maintain the Shi'a mujahidin's capacity to resist any Soviet offensive, without allowing them to attack the Soviets. This policy succeeded in restraining the Soviets from intervening more frequently on the Iraqi side but had very negative side effects in Afghanistan: The Shi'a seemed to be excluded from the jihad. The result was that the Sunni became frustrated and felt that they alone were bearing the brunt of the war effort. Deprived of weapons, the Nasr and Sepah began (mainly from 1986 on) to plunder Sunni arms convoys.

Third, the Iranians had a restrictive policy toward Sunni groups fighting on their borders, in particular the Jam'iyyat. They were rarely authorized to bring weapons from Pakistan through Iran. In 1986, it was forbidden to export any goods from Iran to Afghanistan, thus depriving the mujahidin of food and medicine. Some mujahidin commanders went so far as to say that Iran in fact was playing the Soviet card.

The coherence of Iranian policy was also hampered by the factionalism within Iran's government. After the fall of Mehdi Hashemi, Montazeri's secretary, in Qum (1986), Afghan affairs were simultaneously treated by the Ministry of Interior, which followed the same policy as Qum, and the Ministry of Foreign Affairs, which advocated a more balanced and open policy.

Another obstacle was the opposite evolution of Sunni and Shi'a Islamism. The condition for "Islamism" (that is, political Islam) to take root in Afghanistan is that it must adjust an urban revolutionary ideology to a traditional segmented society. Among Sunni, the Jam'iyyat generally succeeded, whereas the Hizb has failed, in adapting to traditional society. The task was in fact more complicated for Shi'a parties than for their Sunni counterparts. Opposition in central Hazarajat between backward peasants and young clerics returning from Najaf is stronger than between Sunni peasants from the Panjshir Valley and students from Kabul. Hazara peasants used to be more conservative than were peasants elsewhere in Afghanistan. Hazara students, however, usually had radical views.

Despite condemning Pakistan's pro-Western policies, Iran never tried to challenge Pakistani control over Afghan-Sunnis, but only asked for reciprocity. A de facto division occurred: the Sunnis remaining in Peshawar, the Shi'a in Qum. The Pakistanis avoided interfering in Shi'a affairs; officially there were, until 1986, no Shi'a offices in Peshawar (they were established in Quetta), and Pakistan avoided openly supporting a Shi'a faction (although Islamabad indirectly supported some Hazara nationalist secular groups, like Ittihad'yya and Tanzim). This de facto division created many logistical problems both for the Jam'iyyat, which was established at the Iranian border and was generally not allowed to bring weapons from Pakistan through Iran, and for Nasr, for whom the reverse was true. This led to the existence of two different alliances in Peshawar and Qum.

Until mid-1988, Tehran kept the same hard-line policy toward Afghanistan. But in the aftermath of the Iran-Iraq War, Tehran proceeded to an overall reassessment of its foreign policy: The exportation of revolution was seen as a failure. Differences occurred between Iranian "radicals" and "moderates," but a new trend emerged: Tehran sought to participate in the negotiation process and wanted Afghan Shi'as to have a share in any political solution in Kabul. After the Soviet withdrawal of February 1989, Tehran's priority became to forestall the establishment in Kabul of an overall Sunni fundamentalist government.

* * * * * * * *

Sunnis and Shi'a, moderates and radicals, Arabs and Iranians, Western humanitarian organizations, and a cluster of sovereign states (Saudi Arabia, Iran, Pakistan, the former Soviet Union, and the United States—to name only the most prominent) have all played a role in the complex internationalization of political Islam in Afghanistan. These many outside links have obviously had their impact on Afghan life, but it has also been suggested in this chapter that they have, perhaps even more, simply adapted to the essential dynamic of Islam and society in Afghanistan. The issues of continuity and change in Afghanistan itself are more directly addressed in the following chapter.

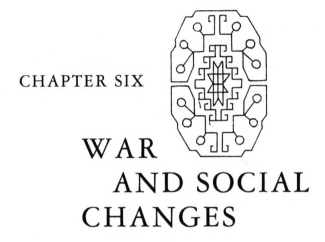

CHAPTER SIX

WAR
AND SOCIAL
CHANGES

THE WAR HAS ALTERED the social as well as the ethnic fabric of Afghanistan.

While qawm affiliation rules the political game at the grassroots level, ethnicity, not the confrontation between Islam and secularism, is now the dominant stake in the contention for central power.

The present war is reshaping ethnic identities. Larger ethnic entities, based on linguistic criteria, have developed, crosscut only by the Shi'a/Sunni dichotomy. Persian-speaking but Shi'a, the Hazara would never call themselves Tajik. Yet, the bulk of Sunni Persian-speakers have now adopted this term, "Tajik," which has been bestowed on them by ethnologists and journalists, and they are developing a sense of community.

For instance, before the war, the people of Panjshir Valley never called themselves Tajik. If asked about the identity of their qawm, they named the solidarity group at the lowest social level, then the village name, then "Panjshiri" (in apposition to Andarabi, Badakhshi, Khosti, etc., all place names), and finally "farsiwan" (Persian-speakers). Tajik was a term used by them to designate a subgroup of Persian-speakers, mainly inhabitants of Badakhshan, who had no other ethnonym, such as Baluchis, Sayyids, Arabs, etc. (in Badakhshan, all these groups speak Persian exclusively). "Tajik" was once used as a qawm appellation rather than as a linguistic or ethnic one. This has now changed. Migrations due to the war, the necessity to coalesce into larger groups in order to achieve political weight, usage imposed by anthropologists and journalists—all these factors have pushed people to identify themselves with large ethnic groups: Pashtun, Tajik, Baluchi, Turkmen, Uzbek, and even Nuristani. For instance, the "Khorasan" refugee camp near Peshawar has brought together

Persian-speakers from different qawms, areas, and ethnic groups; but confronted with the local Pashtun population and refugees, they tend to call themselves "Tajik." The choice of term has not been spontaneous. It was used by anthropologists, Soviet or American, to designate most Sunni Persian-speakers and was then adopted by journalists, notably those working the BBC broadcasts in Persian; the latter are highly respected in Afghanistan.

This process of "ethnicization" did not begin in 1979. Its roots are to be found in the creeping politicization of Afghan society since the 1960s, spearheaded by the Kabul government, which stresses Pashtun nationalism, and by external factors, such as the creation of the Soviet republics of Central Asia, all based on an ethnic group (Turkmen, Uzbek, Tajik). This process had been noticed by anthropologists before the Afghan War. For example, some Turkish-speaking groups used to retain their name and identity (that is, in the sense of the term qawm), such as the Qarluq of Rustaq, but would call themselves Uzbek in addressing other people.[1]

Other groups like the "Tatar" of Doâb-i Ruy (Samangan Province), although retaining an oral tradition of being of Turkic origin, speak Persian exclusively and were formerly considered Tajik[2]; but in 1987, feeling ignored by the Peshawar-based parties, they joined a "pan-Turkic" group, the Ittihad-i Islami-yi vilayât-i samt-i shamal-i, headed by Azad Beg, who at that time was receiving weapons from Pakistani military intelligence.[2]

The dominance of the ethnic factor was clearly demonstrated when in March 1990 Shanawaz Tana'y, Minister of Defense and a staunch Communist, attempted a coup d'état against his Communist colleague President Najibullah, and this was done in alliance with the Islamist radical Gulbuddin Hekmatyar, whom he joined after the failure of the coup. Both Tana'y's and Hekmatyar's men are Pashtun supremacists.

Even so, the ethnicization of the political game along linguis-

1. See Pierre Centlivres, "Les Ouzbeks du Qataghan." This paper is one of the most informative on Uzbek ethnic identity in Afghanistan.
2. Personal observation, August 1987.

tic (and religious) cleavages has not put an end to the traditional
rules of the power game, although it is now played by new actors.
The new elite, brought up by the mujahidin movement, does
not express ethnic claims in terms of nationalistic ideologies (as
in the former Yugoslavia or, more closely, in former Soviet republics). They share the same conception of politics (competition
based on patronage) as the traditional notables, khan, and malik,
but in a rather different context, where competition for power
among contenders is based on foreign interferences and on international networks that circulate foreign goods.

The war brought about the decline of traditional elites (the
Pashtun aristocracy of tribal origin) and the emergence of new
elites—Islamist intellectuals, mullahs, and petty war chiefs
within Afghanistan, on one hand, and, on the other, educated
youths who joined the emigration to Pakistan, all of them people
owing their social advancement to the war and some of whom
became war entrepreneurs, living by and off the war.

How does a "new notable" establish his power? Not as a
feudal lord or warlord, using his military power to take possession
of a part of the agricultural production, but rather as a "redis-
tributor." The new notable creates a network of clients,
strengthened by matrimonial bonds, thanks to the goods he is
able to distribute. These goods do not come by extorting from
peasants, but from international sources. At first, it was a question
of military and financial aid given for political reasons (mostly
from the United States and Saudi Arabia) and also of humanitarian
aid, and then, more recently, profits from marketing weapons
and drugs (opium). Thus, the new powerbase had its origins with
political parties and was strengthened by the fact that the war
and the distribution channels became internationalized.

A new segmentation arose around these new centers of power.
The Islamists took advantage of a modern political structure, the
parties, to entrench themselves and attempt to go beyond the
qawm, clan, tribe, and ethnic group in which the power of
notables was traditionally rooted. The political parties modified,
without supplanting, qawm networks and criteria for identity.
Political modernism has not evolved out of this; rather, these

changes have transformed traditional forms of segmentation and power into a new system.

In the beginning, the Afghan resistance, though it often expelled senior traditional notables, operated according to Afghan society's traditional segmentation by qawm; this led to the proliferation of "local commanders" sometimes at the head of no more than a few dozen fighters who maintained their independence from more important commanders by joining a rival party from which they drew enough subsidies to maintain their status. We have noted the link between the mujahidin's military immobility and the fact that the geography of networks and territories was perceived as "natural" by their protagonists. A "commander" rarely sought to eliminate a qawm that had acquired political expression by joining a party opposed to his own.

In a second phase, the chiefs spawned by the war took over the notables' own manner of exercising power. They established a network of clients, now rendered possible because these chiefs could redistribute acquired assets by entering international channels (input: arms, subsidies; output: drugs and, again, arms), which spared them from becoming predators on their own society. They were distributors. Political learning tended to be structured according to the qawm's manner of operation—by matrimonial alliances, exchanges of gifts, nepotism, etc. New "qawms" were seen to arise, based on centers of power and goods, and these were not always simply an expression of an old qawm. The old segmentation, including the feature of ethnic identities, tended to be reorganized around new centers of power.[3]

What has taken place in Afghanistan is a translation of traditional patterns of power into a society whose fabric has been altered by a modern war and the brutal "internationalization" of even local conflicts between two mujahidin commanders. The fact is that now a conflict in Hazarajat between radical and modern Shi'a, in Pech Valley between traditional tribal leaders and "Wahhabis," or in Helmand Province for the control of a drug

3. On all these very complex data, see O. Roy, "Ethnies et politique en Asie centrale."

market, has international significance. There is no more political autarchy at the local level.

The new patterns of power lasted, however, only as long as the conflict remained internationalized. In fact, the possession of power within a political party gave access to a new asset—arms, sometimes accompanied (for the strongest commanders or those most clever in public relations) by the arrival of humanitarian and financial aid from abroad. Often a right-hand man jealous of his chief would open a front as one might open a shop. Then, to attract a "clientele," he had to give not just arms, but also humanitarian aid: the "French doctor," for example, became a political medium of exchange. The local chief had to agree to take charge of the civil population.

In short, the entry of the Afghan guerrilla into modern political structures has created new notables who act according to the traditional model of exercising power through distribution but whose existence implies new distributive resources and a modern political space: that of political parties and the geostrategy of states. This is particularly evident in the refugee camps, the scene par excellence of social uprooting but nevertheless functioning, thanks to the Pakistani state and foreign aid, as a producer of new notables.

The problem for the authorities in charge of refugees is to find an interlocutor, a counterpart. Pakistani authorities used to deal with traditional malik, entrusting them to distribute the "passbooks" that give people access to subsidies. The United Nations authorities, rightly suspecting that the malik might use this prerogative to enhance his own power (and wealth), decided to create their own administration. The United Nations and NGOs (non-government organizations) acted as a surrogate state. By employing young, educated, English-speaking agents, they promoted a new political elite. Yet, instead of creating a modern administration, they merely allowed power to shift from a traditional elite to a new one that works along the same patterns of clientelism. This intelligentsia is usually more politically minded than the traditional malik. They are closer to the Islamist parties or at least more prone to follow a neofundamentalist ideology, largely spread through a recently established system of schools and scholarships under Saudi or Muslim Brothers patronage. In fact, educated English-speaking interlocutors for Western aid agencies are more readily found in radical fundamentalist groups than in traditional religious schools or tribal milieux.

The mujahidin parties in Peshawar also used international help to build a huge and inefficient bureaucracy, whose sole purpose is to provide jobs for a constituency and to show the strength of their respective parties. Here we find a consistent pattern of Islamism and neofundamentalism. These ideologies go along with a certain modernization of society even if not in the best aspects. They are a factor of centralization and bureaucracy.

The sociological mutation Afghanistan experienced because of the war (new actors transforming traditional power structures into political parties and a new bureaucracy) was rendered permanent by the international context. The participants, not always aware of it and never in control of the process, saw their actions inscribed in a world-wide geostrategy—between fundamentalism and secularism, Shi'ism and Sunnism, Muslim Brothers and Wahhabis, between producers and consumers of drugs, etc. The flow of goods provided by international aid (arms, money, humanitarian aid) profoundly altered and monetarized a rural economy theretofore relatively autarchic. Networks through which the goods and money are distributed, however, have become independent of their political godfathers. Today, many chiefs earn money from drug production—an international trade commodity by definition since little is consumed within the country. Contraband weapons, drug production, and the resulting corruption have made these new economic networks no longer dependent upon a political decision by foreign powers (United States, Russia, or Saudi Arabia) to extend or withhold aid to their allies in Afghanistan. The multiple power centers created by the war have now become relatively independent and now determine the direction of the flow of goods.

Geopolitical factors beyond the control of Afghan actors are changing Afghan society, yet are also encouraging a return to traditional ways and political immobility.

It is consequently striking that the politicization of traditional society induced in Afghanistan as much by the war as by

Islamism has produced only a single truly modern form of politico-military organization. We would call this the Massoud model, so named for the most effective and most modernizing of the mujahidin leaders. It would, of course, be premature to generalize by concluding that Islamist discourse has, in broad terms, simply rewritten in modern terms traditional forms of segmentation, clientelism, and power. A study of these in greater depth remains to be done.

What, then, remains of ideology? Jihad provides a new elite with a legitimizing discourse, but neither a model of organization nor a new political structure for an embattled society. The model instituted by Massoud must be taken into account, to the extent that it is called upon to play a role in the void created by the disappearance of the U.S.S.R., on condition that the model does not itself fall into the same void.

What is a political party in Afghanistan today? Parties express both a translation of qawm structure into a modern society and the reference to an always elusive state. There is still an ideological legitimacy: jihad and Islam. In Afghanistan, a party, however, is first a collection of networks of personal relationships, based on qawm, geographical origin, and family ties. It is not unusual to see these networks expressing themselves in terms of political factions in order to obtain foreign support. For instance, inside the Jam'iyyat party in Herat Province, there are two networks of mujahidin: The first is centered around the regional and official leader, Ismail Khan, and is rooted mainly in rural areas. Ismail Khan, who established his headquarters just outside the city of Herat, is from Shindand in the province of Farah.

The second network, called the Afzali faction (after the name of its former leader, assassinated in 1987), has its constituency among Sunni inhabitants of the city of Herat, usually well educated, and among refugees in Iran. Both groups are Jam'iyyat, both are Islamist. But the Afzali resented the leadership of an "outsider." They played a more radical and ideological tune than did Ismail Khan, attracting thus an Iranian and, paradoxically, a Wahhabi support. In the entourage of the Jam'iyyat party leader in Peshawar, Rabbani, the Afzali were supported by Nurullah Emad, a former student of the Herat School of Theology and an offspring of a prominent Herat clerical family. Emad has close ties with the Saudis, the Pakistani ISI, and the Muslim Brothers. This allowed him to find substantial support for the Afzali, although the official Jam'iyyat teacher was supposed to be Ismail Khan. Thus, a typical qawm as social opposition has been expressed in political factionalism, which in turn has acquired an international dimension, because of Arab and Iranian endeavors to control the mujahidin.

The ideologization entailed by the war tends to disregard the traditional segmentation of society without providing a real political alternative to it. In fact Islamism, as a political ideology, does not provide the key to understanding society. Its insistence on personal ethics and commitments and its disregard for political institutions represent a rejection of politics as such. Conflicts among Muslims are nearly always expressed in terms of lack of Islam, moral corruption, or plots. These conflicts are regularly called "misunderstandings" (*su'tafahum*) or are attributed to ignorance and foreign plots.[4] Hence, the insistence on the necessity for a party member to act as a Muslim and not as a representative of a specific group. The party amir is significantly urged by the Hizb-i Islami rules not to bestow privileges on the basis of "personal friendship . . . and local or tribal relations" (*mahalî va qawmî*).[5] This means that the actual mechanisms of society are known but denied.

Western political science considers institutions more important than people in organizing a polity. The institution can compensate for individual weaknesses or the individual's lack of moral conviction. Politics thus conceived is not based on the personal virtues of the politicians. In modern Islamist political thought, however, politics not based on moral and religious commitment appears as injustice (*zulm*) or as a base stratagem (*hila*). The domestic enemy is the deceiver, the hypocrite, who

4. *Mas'uliat*, p. 110.

5. Ibid., p. 107; see also "a member of the party's *shura* should express his sincere opinion on the basis of his personal faith, comprehension and conscience" and should "avoid any independent faction inside the party" (p. 98).

leads society to *fitna* (dispute within the community). There is always something incomprehensible in fitna. Why should Muslims be divided among themselves? To deplore the lack of unity is a favorite Islamist chorus. There is no political explanation of divisions and segmentations. The endless succession of splits and reconciliations among the parties' leaders in Peshawar is a symptom of this impossibility to think in political terms.

This does not mean that the rules of the traditional power game are unknown. Not only are they well known, but they are the real levers of action used by those involved. These rules are simply not turned into political concepts. The affirmation that religion and politics (*din wa siyasa*) cannot be differentiated is turned into the exact opposite: The real practice of power has little to do with Islam, even if expressed in Islamic rhetoric.

All Afghan mujahidin commanders or politicians know the ethnic and qawm factors, make use of them, live according to them, but would disagree with any Western analyst who bases his analysis of Afghan society on these concepts. The discrepancy between deeds and words is one factor in the inability of Islamist thinkers to provide a proper and realistic political model. A key to Massoud's success in Afghanistan is that he is one of the few Islamists who avoids moral judgments when analyzing facts.

Political Islam has not bypassed traditional society. There has been a reciprocal reshaping, an alteration of traditional segmentation, its translation into political terms, and the emergence of a new intelligentsia. To what extent has the war wrought a re-Islamization of society?

In fact, this ideologization has had little impact on the peasantry and the mullahs (except the so-called Wahhabis). For example, there are very few references to Ibn Taymiyya among the mullahs, although he provides the common ground shared by Salafis, Wahhabis, and Muslim Brothers elsewhere. Jihad is an individual commitment to replace state law, traditional customs, and tribal code by the shari'a, but the war has not caused the discrepancy between the shari'a on one side and tribal code or traditional customs on the other side to disappear. What has disappeared everywhere but in cities is state law (*qanun*).

People have always acknowledged the difference between shari'a and the tribal code and the fact that they follow the latter rather than the former.[6] There is a political secularism of true believers, especially among tribesmen, but no personal secularism. This political secularism has been referred to by nationalist intellectuals and Communists to legitimize their endeavor to put Islam aside as a political factor, for instance by referring to the parliament as a *jirga*, or tribal assembly. But this does not fit with the common perception, which does not see the de facto secularism of tribal institutions as a contradiction to strict compliance with Islam.

Even so, there has always been tension between Islamic rules and the tribal model, which provides not only the values that define "hero" but also working institutions. Shari'a and Islam also provide values that are theoretically recognized as superior, but confined to a separate category of men, "holy men," "sayyid," but also "mawlawi" (not mullahs, who used to be rather despised in tribal society), but no real institutions. The only institution acceptable for the "mawlawis" should be the shari'a court.

In Ghilzay and eastern Pashtun areas, mullahs have constantly tried to destabilize *pashtunwali* (tribal code) in the name of shari'a.[7] This never happened among Durrani. Ghilzay and eastern Pashtun tribal areas have regularly witnessed messianic, fundamentalist movements headed by mullahs (from Sayyid Barelvi to Khalis), always trying to replace tribal customs by shari'a. One should not extend to the whole of Afghanistan this pattern, which seems confined to the Ghilzay community.

Of course, most of the effort of fundamentalist mullahs and Islamist intellectuals during the war has been to replace traditional institutions, like jirga, by Islamic ones, like shari'a courts and shura, for political decisions. Yet, the practices in these new institutions are not very different from the former ones. What has changed is the leadership and the referents of legitimization,

6. Jon Anderson, "How Afghans Define Their Relations to Islam": "Ghilzay will freely admit to being, in their words, 'bad Muslims' and 'not following the religion [*din*]' " (p. 276).

7. Anderson, p. 278.

as shown, for example, by the infighting between Wahhabis and Hizb-i Islami in the Kunar Valley. What is involved there are tribal segments competing for control of the valley; but now they are headed either by mullahs (Wahhabis) or intellectuals (Hizb) who express their opposition either in ideological or ethical terms ("good Muslims" against "unbelievers"), rather than in terms of "misunderstanding," not to say in terms of tribal rivalries.

Most mujahidin commanders, who are not of high tribal extraction, agree with the change of referents that gives them a new legitimacy. But in fact, even in shari'a courts, in all judgments that concern inter*qawm* relations, the mullahs themselves introduce correctives to the strict application of the shari'a in order to take into account the inter*qawm* balance of power. For instance, the abduction of a woman by a man of another qawm would not be treated as adultery but as an episode of the competition between the two groups. The judgment will be cloaked in Qur'ānic terminology but will be aimed at restoring the balance between the two groups and not at "commanding good and forbidding evil" as the strict Islamic maxim requires. The literal application of shari'a (killing the abductor) would lead to a deadly feud between the two groups, creating disequilibrium—a death with no reciprocity. Settling intermujahidin political feuds through shari'a has proved to be hopeless. While most local ulama are not corrupt and are sincerely eager to promote the shari'a, they never go against qawm and party segmentation. When the qawm political game is mastered by Islamist mujahidin commanders, it is not by using shari'a, but by dealing with qawm in a purely political manner.

Politics thus retains and obeys principles other than Islamic political concepts. The complex mix of traditional segmentation, personal ambitions, emergence of new social groups, and reshaping of traditional segmentation under geostrategic constraints enables the larger linguistic groups to become the prominent components of the ongoing political game.

CHAPTER SEVEN

AFGHANISTAN:
FROM IDEOLOGY
TO ETHNICITY

Is AFGHANISTAN A DISTINCTIVE CASE, isolated from the rest of the Muslim world? It is true that the Islamist movement in Afghanistan presents a characteristic not found elsewhere—it is a peasant movement, thus susceptible to the constraints of traditional society (such as segmentation and tribalism). Other Islamist movements such as those in Egypt, Algeria, or Tunisia are above all urban. Even so, we feel that the Afghan mujahidin movement well represents contemporary Islamism.

The rural aspect of the movement is due above all to the fact that urban militants obliged to flee the cities following the Soviet invasion ended up in the countryside. The leadership at all levels of the major Islamist parties in Afghanistan has the same social origin as that of Islamists in other countries of the Muslim world. Further, the war in Afghanistan has increased urbanization as a result of population displacement, including that of the refugee camps; these camps may be regarded as cities in disguise. Finally, the capture of Kabul by the mujahidin (May 1992) brought the leadership of the parties and their bureaucracies back to the capital. Today, it is truly in the cities that Islamists live to make their mark.

The connection between the Afghan Islamist movement and the rest of the Muslim world is also important in terms of personnel. The presence of thousands of Arab volunteers in Afghanistan and the importance that the Afghan jihad has had in Islamist discourse since 1985 demonstrate effectively that the Afghan War has provided numerous Islamist movements, including first and foremost the radical Algerian Islamic Salvation Front (FIS, from the French "Front Islamique du Salut"), throughout the world with a terrain for both experimentation and training. Since 1985, the Islamist world press has followed the war in Afghanistan. Peshawar has become a center of Sunni Islamist publications destined for Muslim Central Asia. Without doubt, Afghanistan is the best example of the Saudi strategy of mounting an alliance with radical Islamists in order to better counter Iran and to legitimize Saudi ties with the Muslim world. The ambiguous connection among the Saudi state, the Wahhabi clergy, and Islamist radicals seems to have survived even the wrenchings of the Gulf War (1990–91). Afghanistan is a case study of the workings of a network of alliances tying together the Muslim world that often ends up directed against the West. This informal globalization of Islamic networks has also an economic aspect. The traffic in arms and drugs plays a key role in the Afghan-Pakistan frontier, helping to finance many activities of the Pakistani secret service (ISI), which, in turn, patronizes other movements involved in Islamist struggles, such as the mujahidin of Kashmir.

What is taking place today is a homogenization of the world Islamist movement. The Afghan mujahid is in fashion. He provides a model for other militants such as the Algerians, at the very least in terms of dress (uniform of long shirt and full, baggy trousers). He is also a stake in the ongoing game of international politics. Pro-Western at first because he fought against the Soviet empire, the mujahid, according to Islamist militants from Arab countries, must now be made to oppose Western influence. This serves to explain the active battle against Western NGOs (non-government organizations) led by the most radical and most militant Arabs in Peshawar. In this struggle against Western influence in Peshawar, the Saudis have played a major role. They are to be found today at the head of anti-Western and anti-Iranian Islamist struggles. This battle is in turn set within a more general dispute over values and Western culture in Islamist and neofundamentalist circles, including those who are strategically allies of the West, such as the Saudi Wahhabis.

The links between the Afghan mujahidin and the world Islamist movement are also to be seen in daily politics. The ideological references of the Afghan mujahidin, as we have seen, were entirely borrowed from thinkers from other parts of the Muslim world. Thus, one has witnessed among the mujahidin the same political evolution as in the rest of the Muslim world, especially the Arab world. The Islamic state is no longer defined in terms of political concepts (such as shura or amir) but solely in terms of applying the shari'a, and this consists, as we have seen, on matters of personal status, i.e., veiling for women and prohibiting alcohol—in short, to issues of right and custom but not of politics as such. Politics continues to function according to a model that is not Western but traditional, even if within a new social context. To judge by the first measures enacted by the mujahidin following their capture of Kabul in May 1992, the model being sketched in Afghanistan is the same as that found in Saudi Arabia, Sudan, post-revolutionary Iran, and without doubt in the Algeria of the FIS. It is the end of the revolutionary dream of redefining social ties in the name of Islam. Today, it involves only the application of a "shari'a veil" that covers a conservative, capitalist, and socially diverse society.

Postscript: Afghanistan Today (1994)

In this book, we have addressed the two main issues of ethnicity and Islam. How can we assess the latest events in Afghanistan and Central Asia from this perspective? If the general trend is realignment along ethnic lines, which, as we have seen, is the case, does this mean that there is no longer an Islamic factor in Afghan politics? Two conclusions are to be drawn:

    1) The process of ethnic consolidation has halted short of ethnic nationalism;

    2) The remaining Islamic radicalism still active inside Afghanistan has lost its native momentum and is now almost entirely directed by the international networks we have analyzed in Chapter Five.

    Most of the present indigenous political actors inside Afghanistan are the same as those we encountered at the beginning of the war, but their constituencies have evolved. The Peshawar parties, as such, do not play an important role in Afghanistan. Rather, we should now distinguish between the provinces and Kabul.

The provinces remain more stable and peaceful than the capital. The stability of provincial towns is remarkable when compared with that of Kabul: Mujahidin commanders who took the provinces in 1992 are the same who have controlled the areas around Kabul since 1980, such as Ismail Khan in the west, or their offspring, e.g., the son of Hajji Latif, in Kandahar. Interestingly enough, these regional powers are not separatist: They all acknowledge that there should be a central (but weak) government in Kabul, and they keep aloof of the present struggle for power.

In Kabul, there are in 1994 four main military forces fighting for power, splitting and reforming along tactical lines. All these forces have an ethnic base. Massoud is the leader of the Tajiks; Dustom of the Uzbeks; Mazari of the Shi'a. Hekmatyar's supporters are Pashtun. The ethnic consolidation has entailed the emergence of four groups with a claim to play a role at the national level. Smaller ethnic groups (Baluchis, Nuristanis, Turkmen) are out of the game. But this process of consolidation has not led to claims of separatism, ethnic cleansing, or reunification with ethnic kin in neighboring countries. The four groups are fighting for a "new deal" for sharing power in Kabul. Another fact is that the Pashtuns are not united under one banner: Hekmatyar is unacceptable to the Durrani tribal aristocracy, who would prefer a deal with the Tajiks.

How does this ethnic consolidation fit with the emergence of national centers for ethnic identity in Central Asia (Turkmenistan, Uzbekistan, Tajikistan)? There has been no solidarity on the two sides of the borders. The Tashkent government still considers all the Uzbeks living abroad (including those in Tajikistan) as foreign citizens; it has not established territorial claims. The Afghan Turkmen, whose families came to Afghanistan to flee the collectivization of the thirties, have little sympathy for President Nyazov's independent Turkmenistan because it remains the most sovietized Central Asian republic. The Tajiks of Tajikistan, who fled the Communist counteroffensive in the winter of 1992–93, were initially welcomed by the Afghan Tajik population, but Massoud refused to give them any military or political support. These refugees were in fact sheltered either by the Uzbek

Dustom or by Pashtun fundamentalist local leaders (like Commander Choghay). By the way, most of them were appalled by living conditions in Afghanistan. Like the Afghan Pashtun refugees into Pakistan in the eighties, political exodus sometimes makes so-called ethnic brothers realize how different they really are. Ethnic solidarity is not a given fact.

What about Islamic solidarity? Islam is no more a criterion of political alignment in Afghanistan, but Afghanistan is still a showcase for foreign Islamist groups. The stakes are in fact important for them. First, thousands of Islamist militants have been trained in Afghanistan; at the same time, at a time when Islamist movements in the Middle East tended to be split according to national boundaries, the militants in Afghanistan shared an internationalist experience: Kurds, Turks, Algerians, and Saudis used to be incorporated into the same fighting groups. Second, when most Arab states (including Saudi Arabia, which prefers to subsidize its radicals in Afghanistan than to have them at home) suppressed or exiled their militant Islamists, it was important for the Islamists to have some safe places in countries where neither local governments nor foreign powers could crackdown on their bases. Third, these Islamist networks need common causes to mobilize the umma: Afghanistan could provide such a common cause. But to achieve these objectives, they needed a clear-cut victory of their friends in Afghanistan, or at least a coalition government that could show how Islam could transcend tribal and ethnic differences. This has not been the case.

These Islamist groups put great pressure on the Afghan mujahidin government: In March 1992, Qazi Hussayn Ahmad, leader of the Pakistani Jama'at-i Islami, and Mustafa Mashhur (a Saudi Wahhabi envoy) came to Kabul in order to convince Massoud to accept the Islamabad Accords, signed by Hekmatyar and Rabbani under Pakistani and Saudi auspices. According to these accords, Hekmatyar was to be promoted to Prime Minister and Massoud demoted to Defense Minister.

All the activities of the Saudi and other Arab envoys inside Afghanistan in 1993 showed that the lessons of the Gulf War were ignored. Islamist radicals enjoy not only the support of the Muslim Brothers, but also of Saudi and Pakistani circles. This support was concealed by the official decision of the Pakistani government to expel Arab activists from Peshawar in April 1993; but the Pakistani political leadership, embroiled in bitter quarrels between President Ishaq Khan and the Prime Minister, Nawaz Sharif, was not really in charge of Afghan policy.

The policy of the "Islamist joint venture" aimed to give Hekmatyar a prominent, but not exclusive, position in Kabul and to establish a bridgehead toward Central Asia in northern Afghanistan. The area of Kunduz, not Kabul, became the hub of radical activities directed toward recruiting Tajik refugees.

But, as we have seen, there is a growing discrepancy between activism of foreign fundamentalist circles and the actual rules of the power game in Afghanistan. The same applies in Central Asia: The Tajikistan crisis is less a matter of Islam vs. Communism· than the expression of a long-time opposition among districts (what the Tajiks call "localism" or *mahalgera'y*). Afghanistan is not an Islamist bridgehead towards Central Asia, even if it remains a zone of anarchy and crisis, spurred by drug trafficking.

Afghanistan, which has never been controlled by a foreign power, cannot be ruled from outside by an "Islamist joint venture." Far from being a starting point for a new Islamist activism, Afghanistan is rather a minefield for international ideological movements. Engulfed in a game of power, Afghanistan has managed to elude any international alignment based on ideology alone.

GLOSSARY OF POLITICAL PARTIES
AND RELIGIOUS ORGANIZATIONS

In Afghanistan

Harakat-i Islami: Shi'i moderate Islamist group led by Shaykh Asaf Muhseni (not to be confused with Sunni Harakat-i Inqilab-i Islami).

Harakat-i Inqilab-i Islami: A traditionalist and clerical Sunni party, recruiting among local mullahs, mainly Pashtun and Uzbek; headed by Mawlawi Nabi Mohammadi.

Hizb-i Islami-ye Afghanistan (Hekmatyar) (HIH): A radical Islamist Sunni party, headed by Gulbuddin Hekmatyar, a Northern Pashtun and former engineering student.

Hizb-i Islami (Khalis): A splinter group of the former, headed by Mawlawi Yunus Khalis, a Pashtun from Ningrahar Province and a traditional mullah.

Hizb-i Wahdat (Unity Party): A Shi'i party established in 1989, under Iranian auspices, by uniting together all the parties active among the Hazara ethnic group.

Hizbullah: A Shi'i party of Herat Province, headed by Qari Yekdast. Also the name of some small Sunni splinter groups on the Afghan-Iranian borders, created under direct Iranian auspices.

Ittihâd-i Islami (Islamic Union): A strict fundamentalist Sunni party, close to the Wahhabis, headed by Abdul Rabb Sayyaf, a young cleric educated in Saudi Arabia.

Ittihad-i Islami-yi vilayât-i samt-i shamal-i Afghanistan (Is-lamic Union of the Northern Provinces of Afghanistan): A pan-Turkish, nationalist, and secular party, created in Pakistan and headed by Azad Beg.

Ittihad'yya: Shi'ite secular nationalist group among Hazara.

Jam'iyyat-i Islami-yi Afghanistan (JIA): A moderate Islamist Sunni group, headed by Burhanuddin Rabbani, a Tajik from Badakhshan and former Lecturer/Assistant Professor of the Faculty of Theology at Kabul University.

National Islamic Front of Afghanistan: Recruits among the former tribal and secular establishment; Sunni, Pashtun, and especially Durrani; headed by Pir Sayyid Gaylani.

National Salvation Front: A small Sunni party headed by a respected clerical figure, Sibghatullah Mojaddidi, educated in Cairo.

People's Democratic Party of Afghanistan (PDPA): The Communist party that took power in April 1978 and lost it in May 1992.

Sazman-i Nasr and **Sepah-i Pasdaran:** Two Shi'i radical Islamist organizations, nowadays merged in the Hizb-i Wahdat.

Shura-yi Inqilabi-yi Ittifaq-i Islami-yi Afghanistan: Traditionalist Shi'ite party founded in 1979. Led by Sayyid Beheshti with recruits from Hazara peasantry.

Tanzim: A small secular Hazara organization, based in Quetta (Pakistan) and created under Pakistani auspices.

Foreign Organizations

Ahl-i Hadith: Founded in the early nineteenth century in the Indian subcontinent; it follows the thought of Shah Waliullah, a reformist thinker of the eighteenth century. This association has turned into a political party in Pakistan and is close to the Saudi Wahhabis.

Jama'at-i Islami: A Pakistani Islamist party, founded in 1941, by Abu al-Ala Maududi. Its headquarters are in Lahore and its present leader is Qazi Hussayn Ahmad. The Jama'at was close to President Zia al-Haqq (1977–88).

Jama'at al-Tabligh: A Muslim missionary society, founded in 1926 and based in the Indian subcontinent. Fundamentalist but never involved in politics, it is involved in grassroots re-Islamization of ordinary Muslims.

The Society of Muslim Brothers: Founded in Egypt in 1928 by Hasan al-Banna, this association has branches in most of the Arab countries. A mix of a political party and of a sociocultural association, it has shaped the thought and the organizational framework of most of the mainstream Islamist organizations in the world. Its center is in Egypt.

Wahhabi: A reformist and scripturalist sect born in Saudi Arabia in the eighteenth century, it is nowadays the official religious school of thought in Saudi Arabia.

BIBLIOGRAPHY

Afghan News, edited by Muhammad Ishaq (Peshawar until 1992; then Kabul).

Ahmad, Qeyamuddin. *The Wahabi Movement in India* (Calcutta: Firma K. L. Mukhopadhyay, 1966; reprinted in Pakistan by National Book Foundation, 1979).

Ahmed, Akbar. *Millennium and Charisma among Sawt Pathans* (London: Routledge and Kegan Paul, 1976).

———. *Pushtun Economy and Society: Traditional Structure and Economic Development* (London: Routledge and Kegan Paul, 1980).

Al-Jihâd (in Arabic, no. 56, Peshawar, June 1989), text of Abdullah Ezzam.

Anderson, Jon. "How Afghans Define Their Relations to Islam," in M. Nazif Shahrani & Robert L. Canfield, eds., *Revolutions & Rebellions in Afghanistan: Anthropological Perspectives* (University of California, Berkeley, 1984).

Arjomand, Said Amir. *The Turban for the Crown: The Islamic Revolution in Iran* (New York: Oxford University Press, 1988).

Azoy, G. Whitney. *Buzkashi: Game and Power in Afghanistan* (Philadelphia: University of Pennsylvania Press, 1982).

Azzam, Salem (ed.). *Islam and Contemporary Society* (London: Longman, in association with the Islamic Council of Europe, 1982).

Bahadur, Kalim. *The Jama'at-i Islami of Pakistan: Political Thought and Political Action* (New Delhi: Chetna Publications, 1977).

Carré, Olivier. *Mystique et politique: lecture révolutionnaire du Coran par Sayyid Quṭb, frère musulman radical* (Paris: Presses de la Fondation nationale des sciences politiques, Editions du Cerf, 1984).

Carré, Olivier et Gérard Michaud. *Les Frères musulmans: Egypte et Syrie, 1928–1982* (Paris: Gallimard: Julliard, 1983).

Centlivres, Pierre. *Un bazar d'Asie centrale; forme et organisation du bazar et Tāshqurghān (Afghanistan)* (Wiesbaden: Ludwig Reichert Verlag, 1972).

———. "Les Ouzbeks du Qataghan," *Afghanistan Journal* (Graz, Austria, 1975).

———. "Les tulipes rouges d'Afghanistan," in Jacques Hainard et al., *Les Ancêtres sont parmi nous* (Neuchâtel, Switzerland: Musée d'ethnographie, 1988).

Charnay, Jean Paul. *L'Islam et la guerre: de la guerre juste à la révolution sainte* (Paris: Fayard, 1986).

Dekmejian, R. Hrair. *Islam in Revolution: Fundamentalism in the Arab World* (Syracuse: Syracuse University Press, 1985).

Dupree, Louis. "Tribal Warfare in Afghanistan and Pakistan," in Akbar S. Ahmed and David M. Hart, eds., *Islam in Tribal Societies: From the Atlas to the Indus* (London: Routledge and Kegan Paul, 1984).

Edwards, David B. "Shi'a Political Dissent in Afghanistan," in Cole, Juan R. and Nikki R. Keddie, eds., *Shi'ism and Social Protest* (New Haven: Yale University Press, 1986).

al-Hâshimi, Abid Tawfiq. "Nizam-i siyasi dar Islam" [Political Order in Islam], a series of articles appearing in 1986 in the monthly *Misâq-i Khûn* (Peshawar).

Hedayetullah, Muhammad. *Sayyid Ahmad: a study of the religious reform movement of Sayyid Ahmad of Râ'e Barelī* (Lahore: Sh. Muhammad Ashraf, 1970).

Hekmatyar, Gulbuddin. *Clues to the Solution of the Afghan Crisis* (Directorate of International Affairs, Peshawar, November 1988).

Hizb-i Islami-ye Afghanistan (Hekmatyar). *Mas'uliat-há-ye 'ozu* [Members' responsibilities].

Iran Yearbook 1989–90 (Bonn: Medien & Bucher, 1990).

Jam'iyyat-i Islami of Afghanistan. *Osûl-e Ba'yat va Mas'uliat-há-ye 'ozu* [The Principles of the Oath of Allegiance and the Responsibilities of the Member], 10th ed., Hamal 1360 (March/April 1981).

———. *Misâq-i Khûn* (a monthly appearing in Peshawar since 1980).

Kepel, Gilles. *Le prophète et pharaon: les mouvements islamistes dans l'Egypte contemporaine* (Paris: Editions La Découverte, 1984).

Kepel, Gilles and Richard Yann (eds.). *Intellectuels et militants de l'islam contemporain* (Paris: Editions du Seuil, 1990).

Khalilzad, Zalmay. "Iranian Revolution and Afghan Resistance," in Martin Kramer, ed., *Shi'ism, Resistance, and Revolution* (Boulder, Colo.: Westview Press, 1987).

Khomeini, Ruhollah. *Pour un gouvernement islamique* (Paris: Fayolle, 1979).

Kopecky, Lucas-Michael. "The Imami Sayyed of the Hazarajat," in *Folk* (Copenhagen: Journal of the Danish Ethnographic Society, 1982).

Maududi, Abu al-Ala. *Jihâd in Islâm* (Beirut: Holy Koran Publishing House, 1980).

Metcalf, Barbara Daly. *Islamic Revival in British India: Deoband, 1860–1900* (Princeton: Princeton University Press, 1982).

The Mirror of Jihâd (March/April; May/June, 1982).

Mortimer, Edward. *Faith and Power: the Politics of Islam* (London: Faber and Faber, 1982).

Poullada, Leon B. *Reform and Rebellion in Afghanistan, 1919–1929: King Amanullah's Failure to Modernize a Tribal Society* (Ithaca, N.Y.: Cornell University Press, 1973).

Qutb, Sayyid. *Fi Zilâl al-Quran* [In the Shade of the Qur'ān] (Cairo: Dār al-Suruq, 1978).

Rifae, Abdullah al-. "Afghan Mujahedeen Fight to Defend their Faith, Country," *Arab News* (Jeddah: Saudi Research and Marketing Company, September 14, 1985).

Roy, Olivier. *Islam and Resistance in Afghanistan* (Cambridge: Cambridge University Press, 2nd ed., 1990).

———. "Les Frontières de l'Iran," in *Revue de la Mediterranée et de l'Occident Musulman*, Aix en Provence, France (Winter 1988).

———. "The Lessons of the Soviet-Afghan War," *Adelphi Paper* (International Institute of Strategic Studies, no. 259, 1:1991).

———. "Ethnies et politique en Asie Centrale," *Revue du monde musulman et de la Méditerranée*, Aix en Provence, no. 59–60 (1–2, 1992).

———. *The Failure of Political Islam* (Cambridge, Mass.: Harvard University Press, 1994).

Shadid, Mohammed K. "The Muslim Brotherhood Movement in the West Bank and Gaza," *Third World Quarterly* 10 (April 1988): 658–82.

Shahrani, M. Nazif. "Local Knowledge of Islam and Social Discourse in Afghanistan and Turkistan in the Modern Period," in Robert L. Canfield, ed., *Turko-Persia in Historical Perspective* (Cambridge: Cambridge University Press, 1991).

Sivan, Emmanuel. *Radical Islam: Medieval Theology and Modern Politics* (New Haven: Yale University Press, 1985).

Tawana, Sayyid Muhammad Musa. "Jonbesh-hâ-ye-Islâmi dar pîch-e wakhm-e târikh" [Islamic Movements in the Turmoil of History], in *Misâq-i Khûn*. 6/7 1360 (1981).

Wâqed, Qâzi Amin. "Hukumat-e Ayande-ye Afghanistan" [The Future Government of Afghanistan] (Section of Predication and Guidance of the Central Office of the Mujahidin Union of Afghanistan, Tehran, 1990).

INDEX

Abdul Rabb Rassul (slave of the Lord of the Prophet), 87
Abdurrasul (slave of the Prophet), 87
al-Afghani. *See* Jamal al-Din al-Afghani
Afghan News (JIA newsletter), 43n, 59, 86
Afghan War, 70, 75, 79, 106
   media coverage of, 70n
Afghans, land of the, 67
Afridis (tribe), 24n
Afzal, Mawlawi, 46, 82
Afzali faction, 111–12
Afzali, Safiullah, 98
ahkâm, 55
ahl al-hall wa al-'aqd (those able to bind and loose), 53–54
Ahl-i Hadith (The People of the Hadith), 20, 46, 81–83, 87, 91, 126
ahl-i tahqâ or *mohaqîq* (of those who are seeking truth), 51
Ahmad, Qazi Hussayn, 80, 123, 127
Aimaq (area), 23n, 24, 92
Akbari, 97
Akora (Pakistan), 82
Alam Khan, 89
"Al-Afghani." *See* Tayyib "Al-Afghani"
Al-Bay'at (book by Abu al-Ala Maududi), 48
Algeria, Algerians, 11, 89, 91, 119, 120, 121, 123
Ali, Sayyid, 83
Al-Jihâd (journal), 46, 86
Al-Usra (family), 48n
Amanullah, 33
Amin, Qâzi. *See* Wâqed, Qâzi Amin
amir, 12, 35, 45, 47, 48, 50–53, 55–57, 59, 80, 112, 121
amir al-mu'minin (commander of the faithful), 35
amirates, 82
Arab News, 86n

Arab volunteers, 88–89 , 119
arbab (landowners), 93, 96
Argo (district), 46, 82, 83
Aristotle, 37
Asadabad, 83
askar (professional soldier), 68–69
Attok, 82
ayatollahs, 40, 93
   grand, 52
al-Azhar University, 44, 85

Badakhshan (province), 23, 46, 82, 105, 126
Badakhshi, Badakhshis, 82, 105
Badmuk, 82
Baghlan, 71
Balkh, 81
Balkhi, Sayyad Ismail, 94
Baluch, Baluchi, Baluchis, 23, 105, 122
Baluchistan, 23
bandit of honor, 71
Banna, Hasan, al-, 11, 12, 13, 20, 29n, 34, 44, 48n, 87, 127
Barelvi, Sayyid Ahmad, 81, 114
Barelvis, 32
Barg-i Matal, 46, 82
Bashir Khan, 71
Ba'thism, 84
Baz, Shaykh ibn, 83, 90
BBC Persian Service, 97, 106
Beg, Alsan, General, 90
Beg, Azad, 106, 126
Beheshti, Sayyid Ali, 94, 96, 126
Behsud, 97
British, 33, 63, 81
   rule in India, 81
Brothers. *See* Muslim Brothers

Cairo, 29, 44, 46, 85, 126
caliph, 50, 51, 53n

Central Asia, 32n, 45, 73, 88, 91, 106, 120, 121, 122, 124
Central Council (*shura-ye markazi*), 48, 49, 54, 55
Central Intelligence Agency (CIA), 79
central units, 73, 74
chiefs, 12, 69, 71, 75, 107, 108, 110
Choghay, Commander, 123
Christianity, 34
CIA. *See* Central Intelligence Agency
Clausewitz, Karl von, 67, 68
commanders, 113
    local, 108
Communist, Communists, 30, 95, 96, 97, 106, 114, 122, 126
    coup of 1978, 29, 33, 49, 50, 67, 95
    party, parties, 12, 49, 126
    regime, 13
community of the pure, 47
Council of Ulama (Saudi), 83, 90

Dahlavi, Abdul Aziz, 81
Danushi, 83
Daoud, President Mohammad, 34
Daoud, Prince, 88
da'wa (preaching Islam), 56
Da'wat-i Islami (Islamic Preaching), 30n
Dawlat (Islamic State of Afghanistan), 82
Deoband (India), 19, 82
Deobandi school, 32
drugs, 91, 107, 108, 110, 120, 124
Durrani, Durranis (Pashtun), 24, 88, 114, 126
    tribal aristocracy of, 122
Dustom, General, 122, 123

Egypt, 11, 20, 30, 31, 38, 44, 46, 57, 79, 85, 119, 127
Eight-Party Alliance, 97
El Souk, 89
Emad, Nurullah, 111–12
Ethnic, ethnicity, 13, 14, 24, 30, 105, 106–7, 123

Ethnic groups, 21–24, 67, 72
    Aimaq, 23n, 24
    Hazara, 23
    Sunni, 23n
Executive Committee, 48
Ezzam, Abdullah, 46n, 85, 86, 88

Faculty of Theology, 20, 44, 46, 80, 85, 126. *See also* Kabul University
Farah (province), 111
farsiwan (Persian-speakers), 24, 88, 105
Faysal, Prince Turki ibn, 84, 87
Fi Zilâl al-Quran, 29n, 44
FIS (Islamic Salvation Front). *See* Front Islamique du Salut
Four Rightly Guided Caliphs, 34–35, 58
Front Islamique du Salut (Algeria), 13, 89, 90, 119, 121
fundamentalism, fundamentalist, 11, 12, 13, 20, 29, 30, 31, 32, 33, 40, 43, 54, 67, 72, 80, 81, 86, 89, 110, 114, 123, 127
    conservative, 91
    foreign, 80, 88, 124
    modern, 84
    neo-, 43–45, 46, 80, 91, 92, 109, 110
    radical, 110
    reformist, 84
    Sunni, 87, 88, 101
    traditional, 34, 39, 45, 46

Gaylani, Pir Sayyid, 83, 99, 126
Ghazni (incident), 99
Ghilzay, Ghilzays (Pashtun), 24, 63, 88, 114
Giap, General, 73
"Guardians," 95
guerrillas, Afghan, 72, 109
Gulf War, 87, 90, 123

Hakim, Ayatollah, 95

ḥākimiyya, 34, 36, 37
ḥalqa (cell), 48
Hamidullah, Mawlawi, 82
Hanafi, Hanifism, 33, 45, 81, 82, 86
  mullahs, 20
  school of law, 19, 33, 81
  Sunni, 67
Hanbali, 33, 45, 57
  school of law, 33
  Sunni, 53
al-Haqq, General Zia. *See* Zia, General
  al-Haqq
Haqqani, 89
Harakat-i Inqilabi-i Islami (Islamic
  Revolution Movement), 43, 95,
  98, 125
Harakat-i Islami (Islamic Movement),
  45, 95, 97, 125
Hasan al-Banna. *See* Banna, Hasan al-
Hashemi, Mehdi, 100
al-Hâshimi, Abid Tawfiq, 29n, 30n,
  36n, 37n, 53n
Hazara, 21, 23, 45, 72, 93, 94, 95, 97,
  101, 125, 126
Hazara Valley, 72, 74
Hazarajat, 21, 93, 96, 99, 101, 108
Hekmatyar, Gulbuddin, 12, 45, 50, 52,
  54n, 58, 73, 80, 84, 86–91, 98,
  99, 106, 122–25
Helmand (province), 108
Herat (city), 24, 45, 93, 96, 111, 112
Herat Province, 111, 125
Hidden Imam, 59
HIH. *See* Hizb-i Islami-ye Afghanistan
hijra, 66
Hindus, 23n
Hizb. *See* Hizb-i Islami-ye Afghanistan
Hizb al-da'wat, 83
"Hizb Allah," 47
Hizb al-Tahrir, 31
Hizb-i Islami-ye Afghanistan (Hizb-i
  Islami) (HIH), 31, 36n, 43–44, 45,
  49, 50, 52, 54, 55, 56, 57, 75, 80,

  82, 83, 86, 89, 98, 99, 101, 112,
  125
  guidebook (*Mas'uliat*), 49, 55, 57
  hierarchy, 48–49
  membership, 55
Hizb-i Islami (Khalis), 125
Hizb-i Wahdat (Party of Unity), 21, 45,
  96, 97, 99, 125, 126
Hizbullah (Party of God), 29, 34, 35,
  45, 89, 96, 98, 125
  of Lebanon, 29
  Shi'a, 29, 45, 96, 125
  Sunni, 98, 125
al-Hudaybi, Hasan, 37
Husayn, Saddam, 79, 90, 94
Husseyn, Mirza, 94

ijtihâd, 45, 51, 52, 53, 55, 81
al-Ikhwan al-Muslimin (Muslim Brothers), 43
Imams, 37n, 57
India, Indian subcontinent, 32n, 33, 45,
  81, 88, 126, 127
Indo-Pakistani association, 91
intellectuals, intelligentsia, 11, 21, 30,
  107, 109, 113, 114, 115
International Revolutionary Party, 47
Inter-Services Intelligence (ISI), 20, 79,
  86, 87, 88, 89, 106, 112, 120
Iran, Iranian, 11, 13, 20, 21, 24, 29,
  38, 40, 57, 59, 88, 92–102, 112,
  120, 121, 125
  influence in Afghanistan, 20, 98, 99,
  100–101
  Islamist movements in, 40
  Ministry of Foreign Affairs, 97
  policy toward Afghanistan, 96, 98–
  101
Iran-Iraq War, 87, 94, 101
Iranian Revolution of 1979, 13, 31, 38,
  39–40, 45, 57, 84, 87, 94
  and the Shah, 40, 93

Iraq, 13, 21, 94, 100
Ishaq, Muhammad, 43n
ISI. *See* Inter-Services Intelligence
Islam
    ideological, 11
    militant, 11
    political, 11, 12, 14, 20, 29, 40, 55,
        57, 92, 101, 102, 113, 114
    "popular," 19
    revolutionary, 30
    scriptural, 19
    secular, 40
    traditional, 21
Islam and Resistance in Afghanistan (Roy),
    13
Islam vs. Communism, 124
Islamabad, 79, 88, 96, 101
    Accords, 123
Islamic
    constitution, 36, 59
    fundamentalism, 30, 40
    ideology, 38
    order (*nizam-i Islami*), 35, 58
    party, 11, 35, 47, 51
    revolution, 11, 35, 38, 51
    rule, 36
    society, 11, 50, 51, 52, 54, 56, 59
    state, 11, 14, 31, 32, 39, 50, 54
Islamic Legion, 86, 88–89
Islamic Revolution Movement, 38. *See
    also* Harakat-i Islami
Islamic Salvation Front (FIS), 119. *See
    also* Front Islamique du Salut
"Islamic State of Afghanistan," 82
Islamism, 30, 31, 34, 39, 90, 101, 110,
    111, 112
    contemporary, 119
    and modernization, 39
    Shi'a, 101
    Sunni, 88, 101
Islamist, Islamists, 32, 54, 58, 79, 87,
    98, 107, 111, 113
    contemporary, 50
    extremist groups, 90

ideology, 11, 12, 14
intellectuals, 21, 52, 53, 54
militant, 123
moderate, 53, 84
momentum, 14
movements, 39, 40, 51, 52, 79,
    80, 89, 120
parties, 14, 38, 79
radical, 31, 37, 38, 45, 53, 54, 83,
    84, 85, 89, 120, 123, 126
revolution, 13
Shi'a, 43, 45
Sunni groups, 38, 43, 57, 84
Islamization, 14, 20, 30–31, 47
Ismaili mountaineers, 23n
Israeli-Palestinian conflict, 79 .
Ittihâd-i Islami (Islamic Union), 46,125
Ittihad-i Islami-yi vilayât-i samt-i
    shamal-i Afghanistan (Islamic
    Union of the Northern Provinces
    of Afghanistan), 106, 126
Ittihad'yya, 101, 126

Jadrans (tribe), 24n
jâhiliyya, 34, 35, 37, 50
Jaji, Jajis (tribe), 24, 89
Jama'at al-Tabligh, 91, 127
Jama'at University, 80
Jama'at-i Islami, 20, 31, 32, 34, 38n,
    39, 79, 80–81, 87, 91, 123, 127
Jamal al-Din al-Afghani, 34
Jami'at al-Ulama, 80, 98
Jam'iyyat-i Islami-yi Afghanistan (JIA),
    29n, 36, 39n, 43, 44n, 47, 49, 51,
    53n, 56, 57, 66, 72, 74, 80, 82,
    83, 85, 86, 90, 98, 99, 101, 111,
    112, 126
    guidebook (*Osûl-e Ba'yat*), 36n, 38n,
        44n, 45n
    journal (*Misâq-i Khûn*), 29n, 36n, 53,
        59
Jamilurrahman, Mawlawi, 83
Jawanan-i Mosalman (Young Muslims),
    85

JIA. *See* Jam'iyyat-i Islami-yi Afghanistan

jihad, 63, 64, 66–68, 70, 72, 75, 79, 85, 88, 89, 100, 111, 113, 119

Jihad (radical group), 31, 38

Jihâd in Islâm (Maududi), 29n, 35n, 36n, 37n 47n, 53n

Jordan, 20, 31, 38

Jurm, 83

Kabul, 13, 24, 44, 46, 72, 73, 80, 90, 93, 94, 96, 101, 106, 119, 121–24

government, 106

Kabul Radio, 46

Kabul University, 46, 80

Kalafgan, 74

Kâm (tribe), 82

Kandahar, 45, 93, 94, 95, 122

Karachi, 29, 82

Kashmir, 89, 120

Kâtis (tribe), 82

Kerbala, 94

Keshm, 74

Khalifa, Muhammad Abdurrahman, 85

Khalis, Mawlawi Yunus, 44, 99, 114, 125

Khamene'y, Ali, 40n

khan, khans, 25, 65, 67, 71, 75, 92, 107

Khan, Bashir, 71

Khan, Basir, 71

Khan, Ishaq, President, 124

Khan, Ismail, 71, 89, 98, 111, 112, 122

Kheyratmand, 83

Khorasan refugee camp, 105

Khosti, 105

Khugiani (tribe), 24

Khumayni, Ayatollah, 21, 31, 36n, 39, 40, 45, 57, 93, 95

Khuy, Ayatollah, 95

Kizilbash, 21, 93, 95, 97

Koranomunjan, 74

Kunar (province), 46, 82, 83

Kunar Valley, 82, 115

Kunduz, 124

Kurds, 22, 88, 123

Kuwaitis, 90

Lahore, 81, 127

language, as the basis for identity, 23

Latif, Hajji, 122

leaders, leadership, 47, 52, 65

charismatic, 59

tribal, 43

Lebanon, 29

Leninist

organization, 45

party model, 11, 46

tradition, 47

"Liberation Party" (Hizb al-Tahrir), 31

Madina, 40

madrasa, madrasas, 19, 20, 46, 80, 82

traditional, 44

Majlis al-Shura, 48

malik (leader), 25, 107, 109

Maliki, school of law, 33

Mansur, Nasrullah, 98

Mansura (Lahore), 80

Maoist, Maoists, 98

movements, 95

markaz (military base), 70–71

traditions, 71

martyr, martyrs (*shahid*), 69, 70, 97

Marxism, 11

Mashhur, Mustafa, 123

Massoud, Ahmad Shah, 12, 63, 69, 86, 87, 98, 111, 113, 122, 123

military model, 72–75, 111

Mas'uliat (HIH guidebook), 44n, 47n, 48n, 49, 52n, 54n, 55, 57, 58n, 112n

Maududi, Abu al-Ala, 11–12, 13, 20, 30, 34–37, 38, 40, 44, 45, 47, 48n, 50, 52, 53n, 80, 81, 87, 127

Mazari, Shaykh, 95, 97, 122

Mecca, 46, 84

Meshwani Pashtun (tribe), 83

military professionalism, 68–69
milla (nation), 67
Ministry of Foreign Affairs, 100
Ministry of Interior, 100
mir (landowners), 93, 96
Misâq-i Khûn (JIA guidebook), 29n, 36n, 37n, 53n, 59
Mo'azen, Mawlawi, 98
Moghul Empire, 88
Mohammadi, Mawlawi Nabi, 125
Mohaqeq, Qorban Ali, 95
mohaqîq, 51, 52
Mohmands (tribe), 24n
Mohtashemi, 97
Mojaddidi, Sibghatullah, 90, 98, 99, 126
Montazeri, Ayatollah, 96, 100
Moros Liberation Front (Philippines, 89
Moscow, 96
"muhajir" (Uzbek), 83
Muhammad, Prophet, 12, 22, 24, 32, 34, 35, 37, 40, 57, 58, 59, 87, 91, 93
Muhseni, Shaykh Asaf, 94, 95, 96, 97, 125
mujahid, 68–69
  rank and file, 68
mujahidin, 12, 13, 15, 20, 29, 30, 43, 46, 63, 70, 71, 72, 75, 79, 80, 84–86, 88–91, 97–100, 107, 108, 110–13, 120
  of Kashmir, 120
  commanders, 58, 115, 122
mujtahid, 40
mullahs, 12, 20, 21, 22, 31, 46, 51, 64, 65, 82, 84, 91, 97, 107, 113–15, 125
  Afghan, 44, 82, 84
  fundamentalist, 12, 46, 114
  Hanafi, 20, 82
Muslim Brothers, 14, 20, 29–30n, 31, 32, 34, 37, 38n, 39, 43, 44, 46, 48n, 57, 79, 81, 84–90, 92, 99, 100, 110, 112, 113, 123, 127
  in Afghanistan, 44

Egyptian, 30n, 44, 46, 48n, 57, 122
Jordanian branch, 85
Palestinian, 48n
radical, 99
Muslim party, 37

Nabhani, Taqi al-Din, 31
Nader, Haji, 95
Nahrin, 74
Najaf, 93, 94, 101
Najibullah, President, 106
Nasr. *See* Sazman-i Nasr
Nasser, Mawlawi Jamal, 83
Nasserism, 84
Nassif, Doctor Abdullah Omar, 84
National Assembly, 93
National Islamic Front of Afghanistan, 126
National Salvation Front, 98, 126
Nawaz, Sharif, 90
neofundamentalism, 20, 39, 43, 45, 80, 91, 92, 109, 110, 120
NGOs (non-government organizations), 109, 120
Niazi, Gholam, 85
Niazi, M., 44
Nili, 95, 97
Ningrahar (province), 125
Nizâm-i siyasi dar Islâm (Political Order in Islam), 30, 36
Northern Supervisory Council (*shura-ye nazar*), 74
Northwest Frontier (province), 82
notables, 25, 71, 75, 92, 95, 107, 108, 109. *See also* chiefs, khan
Nuristan, Nuristani, Nuristanis, 23, 46, 82, 105, 122
Nurullah Emmat (group), 86
Nuruz Kheyl (name of Massoud's family) 73
Nyazov, President, 122

Obeydullah (leader), 82
opium, 107. *See also* under drugs

Opus Dei, 38
Organization of the Islamic Conference, 79
Osûl-e Ba'yat (JIA journal), 36n, 38n, 44n, 45n, 49n, 51n, 56, 57, 68n, 69n

Pakistan, 24, 33, 46, 69, 80, 81, 82, 84, 88, 91, 92, 100, 101, 102, 107, 126, 127
  Army, 88, 90
  government, 90, 124
Pakistani, Pakistanis, 72, 75, 79, 80, 82, 84, 86, 87, 90, 91, 101, 109, 112, 120, 123, 124, 127
Paktya (province), 89
Palestine, 31, 85, 89
Palestine Liberation Organization (PLO), 69
Palestinians, 85, 89
Pamir, 23n
Pan-Turkish, 106, 126
Panjpir, 82
Panjshir Valley, 72, 101, 105
Panjshiri, Panjshiris, 73, 74
Parachi (language), 74
Party of God. *See* Hizbullah
Paryan Valley, 72
Pasdaran
  Afghan, 95
  Iranian, 96
Pashay, 23n
Pashtun, Pashtuns, 14, 21, 22, 23, 24, 63, 64, 67n, 75, 80, 87, 88, 93, 96, 99, 105, 106, 107, 114, 122, 123, 125, 126
  Durrani, 88
  Pakistani, 24, 80
pashtunwali (law of the Pashtuns), 22, 114
Pathans (Pakistani Pashtun), 24
PDPA. *See* People's Democratic party of Afghanistan
Peasants, Peasantry, 30, 74, 93, 101
  Hazara, 101
  Sunni, 101

Pech Valley, 82, 83, 108
People's Democratic Party of Afghanistan (PDPA), 24, 126
Persian-speakers (*farsiwan*), 24, 57, 87, 88, 93, 96, 99, 105, 106
  Hazara, 105
  Sunni, 23n, 105, 106
Peshawar, 46n, 66, 72, 81, 83, 85, 86, 88, 96, 101, 105, 111, 113, 120, 124
  alliance, 98
  parties, 20, 24, 106, 110, 121
Philippines, 89
Pir, 48, 92
Pir of Obey, 98

Qarabagh (incident), 99
Qarluq of Rustaq, 106
qawm, 21–25, 64, 69, 72, 73–74, 75, 105, 106, 107, 108, 111–13
Quetta, 101, 126
Qum, 94, 96, 97, 100, 101
Qur'ān, Qur'ānic, 11, 20, 33, 35, 37, 40n, 45, 47, 51, 53, 56, 57, 59, 115
Qutb, Muhammad, 29n, 36, 40, 44, 52
Qutb, Sayyid, 11, 12, 20, 29n, 30, 34, 35, 36, 38n, 39, 40, 44, 45, 47, 54, 84, 85

Rabbani, Burhanuddin, 29, 44, 50, 85, 87, 90, 111, 123, 126
Rabita (World Islamic League), 84, 87
radicalism, political, 38
Rassoul, Amir, 71
Rassul, Abdul Rabb, 87
Red Crescent, Saudi, 86
reform, reformist, 81, 127
  movement, 20
  religious, 45
  scripturalist, 32, 43, 84
  sect, 127
  thinkers (*salafis*), 34
refugee camps, 105, 109, 119
rish-e safid (white beards), 65
Riyadh, 83, 85

Russia, 88, 110
Rustam, Mawlawi, 82

Sadat, Anwar al-, 38, 85
Safavid Empire, 93
Safi (subtribe), 24n, 83
salafi, salafis (reformist thinkers), 34, 52,
    82, 113
Salasin Madrasa, 83
Samangan (province), 106
Samarkand, 23
Saud, House of, 84
Saudi, Saudis, 20, 33, 84, 85, 87,
    90, 112, 120, 123. *See also* Wah-
    habi
  Brothers, 20, 89
  dynasty, 33, 84
  government, 83
  monarchy, 90
  Red Crescent, 86
  secret service, 84
Saudi Arabia, 31, 79, 83–85, 98, 102,
    107, 110, 121, 123, 125, 127
Sayyaf, Abdul Rabb, 46, 83, 87, 90, 125
sayyid, (descendant of the Prophet
    Muḥammad), 21, 22, 24, 73, 93,
    105, 114
Sazman-i Nasr (Nasr), 45, 95, 96, 126
School of Theology (in Herat), 111
Scripturalist
  reformist movement, 84
  sect, 127
secularism, secularization, 40, 114
segmentary group (*qawm*), 14, 21, 63
segmentation, 21, 25, 58, 66, 67, 107,
    108, 111
  ethnic, 67, 88
  party, 115
  social, 58
  traditional, 66, 92, 108, 111, 112,
    115
  tribal, 58, 66, 67
Sepah-i Pasdaran (Sepah), 45, 96, 97,
    126

Shadid, Mohammed K., 48n
Shafi'i, school of law, 33
shahid (martyrs), 97
Shahrani, Nazif, 19n
Shahr-i Bozorg, 83
shari'a, 11, 31–35, 39, 40, 43, 51, 54,
    55, 56, 59, 66, 67, 80, 81, 91,
    113–15, 121
Shariat Bill, 81
Shariati, Ali, 45
Shariat-Madari, Ayatollah, 95
Sharif, Nawaz, Prime Minister, 90, 124
Shariqi, Mawlawi, 82–83
Shi'a, Shi'i, Shi'ite, 20, 21, 23, 38, 39,
    67, 84, 88, 92–98, 102, 122, 125,
    126
  Afghan, 21, 97, 99–101
  Hizbullah, 29, 45, 96, 125
  and Iran, 20–21, 94
  modern, 108
  parties, party, 101, 126
  radical, 108
  traditionalist, 126
Shi'a-Sunni dichotomy, 105
Shi'ism, 40, 57, 81, 110
  Iranian, 67
Shindand, 111
Shinwari Pashtun (tribe), 83
Shotol Valley, 72
shura (advisory council), 50, 51, 53, 54,
    56, 112, 114, 121
shura-ye markazi. See Central Council
shura-ye nazar. See Northern Supervisory
    Council
Shura-yi Inqilabi-yi Ittifaq-i Islami-yi
    Afghanistan (Shura), 95, 96, 97,
    126
Siddiqi of Nili, 95, 97
Sikhs, 23n
Society of Muslim Brothers, The, 127
solidarity
  groups (*qawm*), 14, 71, 66, 105
  space, 15, 64, 65, 66, 71, 72, 73,
    74, 75

Soviet, Soviets, 13, 30, 66, 68, 70, 71, 73, 98, 99, 100, 106
    Army, 12, 30
    empire, 120
    invasion (of Afghanistan), 21, 29, 63, 67, 79, 82, 85, 119
    republics, 106, 107
    withdrawal, 79, 101
Soviet Union, 63, 66, 68, 71, 73, 102
Sudan, Sudanese, 20, 99, 121
    relief agencies, 86
Sufi, Sufism, 19, 43, 46, 47, 48, 55, 81, 83, 86, 92
    brotherhood, 11
    Deoband school (India), 19, 32
    marabouts, 46
"Sulayman," 82
Sunna, 20, 35, 51, 56, 81
Sunni, Sunnis, 19, 29, 36, 38, 39, 40, 43, 44, 59, 74, 81, 88, 91, 93, 95, 96, 98, 100, 102, 110, 111, 120, 125, 126
    Afghan, 97, 99
    fundamentalist, 43, 125
    parties, 99
    Persian-speaker, 23, 72, 106
    radical groups, parties, 39, 99, 125
Supreme Council of the Muslim Brotherhood, 87
Syria, 38

Taghadossi (cleric), 95
Tajik, Tajiks, 23, 24, 83, 88, 105, 106, 122, 126
Tajikistan, 122, 124
takfîr (declaring a Muslim to be a non-Muslim), 37, 44
Takfîr (radical group), 38
Talmasani, Shaykh, 44, 57
Taloqan (provincial capital), 74
Tana'y, Shanawaz, 106
Tashkent, 122
"Tatar" of Doâb-i Ruy, 106
Tavasolli, 94

Tawana, Sayyid Muhammad Musa, 30n
Taymiyya, Ibn, 113
Tayyib "Al-Afghani," 89
Tehran, 96, 99, 101
Tehran Radio, 98
Third World liberation movements, 12
Tohfe Asna Ashari'a, 81
traditionalists, 43, 103
tribal, tribalism, tribes, 13, 14, 21, 22, 24, 30, 33, 58, 64, 65, 66, 67, 86, 88, 90, 92, 107, 110, 113, 114, 115
    affiliations, 58
    Afridis, 24n
    confederations, 24
    conflict, 64, 65, 67
    Jadrans, 24n
    Jajis, 24n
    Khugiani, 24n
    Mohmands, 24n
    Pashtun, 88
    Safis, 24n, 83
    traditional, 71, 119
    warfare, 65, 71
    Waziris, 24n
Tunisia, 119
Turabi, Hasan, 99
Turkey, 81
Turki, Saudi Prince. *See* Faysal, Prince Turki ibn
Turkish speakers, 23, 24
Turkman Valley, 95
Turkmen, 23, 105, 106, 122
Turkmenistan, 122
Turks, 88, 89, 123

ulama, 19, 31, 33, 51, 52, 53, 54, 67, 72, 92, 100, 115
    Saudi Council of, 83, 90
umma, 13, 35, 47, 51, 53, 65, 66, 85, 91, 123
United Nations, 92, 109
United States, 33, 89n, 99, 102, 107, 110

Uzbek, Uzbeks, 23, 24, 83, 105, 106, 122, 125
Uzbekistan, 122

velâyat-i faqîh, 40
Voice of America, 46n
volunteers, Arab, 88–89, 119

Wa'ez (cleric), 94
Wahhabi, Wahhabis, Wahhabism, 14, 20, 31, 32n, 33, 43, 45, 46n, 57, 81, 82, 83, 84, 85, 87, 90, 91, 92, 98, 100, 108, 110, 111, 113, 115, 120, 123, 125, 127
    amirates, 46, 83, 84
    Saudi, 14, 81, 120, 123, 127
Waliullah, Shah, 19, 20, 32, 81, 126
Wâqed, Qâzi Amin, 98

warfare, 63–75
    traditional, 63–65, 71–72, 75
Waziris (tribe), 24
"white beards" (*rish-e safîd*), 64
women, and warfare, 70
Working Brother, 48n
World Islamic League, 84. *See also* Rabita

Yekdast, Qari, 96, 125
Young Muslims (Jawanan-i Mosalman), 85
Yugoslavia, 107

Zaher, Ehsan Illahi, 81
Zahir, King, 33–34, 38, 93, 98
Zia, General al-Haqq, 33, 80, 81, 127
zyarat (tombs of holy men), 82